Nathaniel

The Art of Seeing
Your Psychic Intuition, Third Eye, and Clairvoyance

A Practical Manual for Learning and Improving Your Clairvoyant Abilities

First Edition – Updated

astateofmind

www.astateofmind.eu

Copyright © 2012, 2013 Nathaniel
First Edition - Updated

ISBN for print: 978-1477666982

Edited by Joanne Asala
Compass Rose Horizons - http://www.compassrose.com/

Publisher:
A State of Mind (http://astateofmind.eu)
Email: nathan@astateofmind.eu
Wroclaw 2012

Additional Credit:
Primary font for title and A State of Mind's Logo: Fertigo, by Exljbri. Additional font: OptimusPrinceps, by Manfred Klein. Ajna Chakra image:
http://www.flickr.com/photos/dragonflyriri/3475122453/

Table of Contents

The Book of Theory 11

What Is Clairvoyance? 11
Can People See Things? 14
Learning the Basics, or the Fast Guy Guide 18
Things That You Can See 20
Two Types of Seeing 26
Intuitive Sight, Inner Sight 27
Third Eye and Intuition 30
Using Affirmations to Set Up a Foundation 42
Preparing Your Room, Preparing Yourself 51
The Alpha State 58
Psychic Energy Cleansing 61
Summary 63

The Book of Practice 65

The Clairvoyant Laboratory Technique 65
The Psychonaut Method — A Spiritual Journey 72
Do Angels Have Wings? 76
The Clairvoyant Symbols Dictionary 78
Seeing Auras 80
The Chakra Reading 83
Doing Psychic Readings 92
Practicing Clairvoyance Through Observation 97
Practicing Clairvoyance On-Line 100
The Clairvoyance Support Circle 102
Automatic Clairvoyance and Learning Control 104

FREQUENTLY ASKED QUESTIONS	105
SUMMARY	111
APPENDIX A — CORE IMAGES WORK	113
BIBLIOGRAPHY	125

Disclaimer

Psychic abilities take different forms, and an understanding of those psychic abilities takes even more forms. This book presents clairvoyance as I see it — my perspective and tips will fit some of you, but not all of you. Some of you might learn a lot from this book, while others will find it useless. That's because there are many paths that lead to the development of psychic abilities. Those who can already use clairvoyance might be surprised with the content of this book because clairvoyance takes many forms, too. Please, keep these things in mind as you progress with reading.

A Word of Warning Before We Begin

People these days are very interested in paranormal subjects, especially in their practical aspects — psychic abilities are just one example. New Age books and workshops promote esoteric and spiritual techniques of various origins. Books teach communication with spirits and how to channel, as well as energy work of different sorts and such, but do not be blinded by the words of love that many New Age authors promote: remember, where there is Yang there is Yin, as well. Light cannot exist without darkness, and esoteric/spiritual techniques are not 100% safe. As a spiritual worker, you enter a world of both positive and negative entities, energies, and events. Be sure that you want this, and be sure to know how to defend yourself against negative entities. Too many New Age practitioners have fallen into darkness simply because they thought "love speech" would protect them. But you need more than just love speech to survive. No author can take responsibility for depression, possession, obsession, paranoia, or mental and physical problems that may occur on your spiritual path — neither do I. You are a sole creator of your life, but remember, please — spiritual development is fascinating and useful, just keep the safety rules in mind.

This book, as it is, is not meant for total beginners. For those, I've written another book, *Psychic Development Simplified*. It covers the very basics of psychic development from meditation and subconscious mind work to the basics of energy work. If you're a total beginner, please refer to *Psychic Development Simplified*. There are many paths that lead to the development of psychic abilities. There are many schools of thoughts, many systems, many types of workshops and teachers. Choose the one that suits you the most.

The Art of Seeing is meant for people who already practice the basics: they meditate, they work with energies, they re-program their mind and deal with negative patterns such as fears, worries, concerns, bad experiences, and such. Seeing things through clairvoyance, seeing ghosts and spirits and energies like auras, is a complex subject, and, to be honest, *might* be very difficult to learn at first. But once you get the basics, all you have to do is to practice, and things will develop on their own.

It doesn't mean that you can just sit down and wait. Clairvoyance cannot be developed just by practicing clairvoyant exercises — you must keep your general psychic development going; you must keep developing yourself on a spiritual level. Only then will your clairvoyance develop further. It's because energy goes up! If you have ever wondered why it is important to work with all the lower chakras and practice general psychic development before learning clairvoyance, here's the answer. The Third-Eye chakra, which is responsible for clairvoyant perception, requires fuel in order to perceive through clairvoyance. And fuel goes from the lower Tan T'ien — an energy center — through the first five chakras. So you need to develop your psychic abilities and spirituality steadily and gently for a few months, at least, before you jump into practicing clairvoyance. And you need to maintain proper spiritual levels of your personality if you want the ability to function without continual problems.

You might be surprised by seeing that this manual is only 100 pages long, give or take. How can one explain such a complex psychic ability like clairvoyance in such a small book? Well, who told you that clairvoyance is complex or difficult, anyway? The truth is that clairvoyance is a very, very simple ability to learn and work with, at least in theory. It doesn't require too much explaining. On the contrary, I can explain clairvoyance within a few pages, and then provide you with exercises and ways of practicing your new psychic ability — because it's all about practice. The difficulty of the learning process and practice that I've mentioned earlier is caused by forgetting about the basics, or by not being ready to learn clairvoyance in the first place. Keep this in mind, please.

Once you know what to look for, and you know a few basic exercises and techniques for using clairvoyance, everything else is your own practice, mixed with reading books about astral and spiritual planes to gain more theoretical knowledge and keeping your personal journal/dictionary of clairvoyant perception. That's it! And that's why this book is short — there's no need for me to talk too much just in order to get a few more pages, because it wouldn't be honest. Clairvoyance is simple once you know the basics of psychic growth — most people can learn it. The trickiest part will be to understand what "letting go" means and what "inner sight" is — but you will learn this, don't worry.

Finally, remember that this book, even if it contains a lot of theory, has been written from a practical perspective. I'm clairvoyant. I can "see," so I do know what I'm talking about. Now, that's all for the moment. Enjoy the book!

The Book of Theory

You can't learn practical aspects of clairvoyance if you don't learn the theory, first. That is why the first part of this book will explain the theory, but it will also provide you with practical knowledge about affirmations, visualization, and relaxation techniques. Later on, in the second part of this book, you will learn practical exercises that will help you develop clairvoyance.

What Is Clairvoyance?

Clairvoyance is a psychic ability that allows you to see things that are either etherical, i.e., made up from psychic energies, or information received as psychic messages through visual means, as images. When you see things that are real but without physical form, then you are experiencing clairvoyance, an ability to see the unseen. As R. E. Guiley stated in her encyclopedia, clairvoyance is a "paranormal vision of objects, events, places, and people that are not visible through normal sight" (Guiley, p. 95). This skill is used by psychics to perceive etherical beings, such as spirits, ghosts, or angels, or to see energies and to perceive auras, chakras, or cords of psychic energy. Finally, clairvoyance is used by people who perform psychic readings. In that last case, the psychic does not see things that are actually out there, but he perceives information, messages, through "visions." This book is meant to teach you how to see energies, entities, and how to receive psychic messages, because, in the end, all of this is just information. Energy is information, and information is energy.

"Clairvoyance" as a term was created in the late eighteenth century by the followers of Dr. Franz Anton Mesmer, but, of course, the ability to perceive things on different layers of reality is as old as humanity itself — or even older.

The word "clairvoyance" itself is made of two parts: the French words *clair* meaning "clear" and *voyance* meaning "vision." As a psychic ability, clairvoyance is a form of extra-sensory perception, an ability to perceive things by use of the "sixth sense" or, to be more specific, by not using any of your normal five senses. Most people are clairvoyant, since most of the people have sight as their dominant sense. After reading this book and spending a few months practicing daily — or at least twice or thrice a week — there's a great chance that you will be able to use your clairvoyant ability just as you use your hands. It will be natural. If you aren't successful, then either you have spent too little time working on the basics (meditation, energy work, the fundamentals of psychic development) or you're not really clairvoyant and your best "psychic sense" is something other than clairvoyance.

I don't want you to waste your money, so, as long as these words should fit into a free chapter, here's a small test that will generally tell you what your dominant psychic sense is. If your dominant psychic sense is sight, then you WILL develop clairvoyance. Just be careful — no test is perfect, so coming out with clairaudience or clairsentience as a result of the test doesn't mean that you can't learn clairvoyance. To give you an example, I'm clairvoyant, and my primary "normal" sense is sight. But I can also "hear" things. I do have experience in hearing spirits; this tells me that if I would devote some time learning and developing clairaudience, I would be able to use this skill just as I'm using clairvoyance.

Use the test, but decide for yourself if you want to learn and develop your own clairvoyant abilities.

Exercise: Think of a Horse

Indeed, think of a horse.

What did you experience? Did you hear the neigh of a horse? Or did you see an image of a horse in front of your inner eye? Or maybe you smelled a horse? Well, if you saw an image of a horse, then your primary sense for this exercise is sight.

Continue this exercise with the following words: refrigerator, orange, cat, peace, harmony. If you're a visual person, in most cases (not really in all of them), you should see mental pictures as representations of these words. This MIGHT suggest you're a visual person.

In addition, here's something that should help you define if you're a visual person. As *Playful Psychic* states[1]:

Visual people prefer a variety of sights and colors. They prefer pictures full of meaning, written directions, and maps rather than verbal instructions. Visual people say "show

---

1 http://www.psipog.net/activepsy/book1.html#_Toc472931476

me" rather than "tell me." They are able to imagine vivid pictures and scenes. They may imagine colors and pictures when listening to music. They also read books by picturing scenes more than by hearing the words in their heads.

If you can clearly say that you're a visual person, then you can develop clairvoyance easily. But even if you're not really a visual person, you can learn clairvoyance to some degree, and it will act as a support psychic skill. You see, what I've noticed in my own practice is that clairvoyance rarely stands alone. In most cases, it comes along with some level of clairaudience and intuitive work when you simply "know things." Today, when I say that I'm clairvoyant or that someone else is clairvoyant, I mean that clairvoyance is the primary psychic skill that is used to collect psychic information, but in addition, it is supported by other psychic skills that are more or less useful.

Can People See Things?

Can people see things that do not have a physical form? Well, I wouldn't be writing this book if I didn't believe they could. Clairvoyance is a very popular psychic ability, but most people aren't even aware they can see things, which is interesting because most people *are* clairvoyant. I don't want to discuss if clairvoyance is real or not, or whether it is a delusion or a form of hallucination. For the purpose of this book, we assume that we aren't delusional and that we do have the capability to become clairvoyant.

How is it possible that people can see things? Here comes the theory of multidimensional space. According to occult teachings from almost every corner of the world, the universe is made up of a few planes; these include physical plane, etherical plane (energy plane), astral plane, spiritual plane, and few other planes/layers of reality. Different esoteric traditions, from shamanic practices to Christianity to Buddhism, have their own cosmologies that discuss different planes of existence that exist at the same space and time, but in different dimensions. Physical senses can perceive the physical world only, but your spiritual/psychic senses can perceive the other planes that exist here and now. By developing your spiritual senses, you gain access to the etherical, spiritual world around you, and this way, you can perceive the unseen.

In Christian cosmology, we have Hell, Earth, Purgatory, and Heaven. These are the planes of existence. In almost every shamanic tradition, we have the lower worlds where lower spirits exist, the middle worlds (Earth) where humans and animals dwell, and the upper words where gods and higher entities exist. Theosophy, based on Hindu teachings, mentions the physical plane first, our world; then there's the etherical world, the world of psychic energies, life force (Chi, Prana, Ki, Mana; there are different names for life force); next, there's the astral plane where energies and emotions create a mysterious mixture of chaos; higher, there's the spiritual plane where higher beings exist. On all planes, we can find spiritual entities and etherical beings. And these are only a few examples; if you're interested in different esoteric cosmologies, you won't have any problem with finding the proper literature on the market. Now, let's get back to clairvoyance.

Clairvoyant sight seems to be quite popular among people who, one way or another, work with psychic energies — this is not limited to people who call themselves "psychics," and that's why this book is separate from a general how-to psychic development book. But in order to explain it further, we really need to define who's psychic, actually. Basically, what we call psychic development is a set of exercises and principles that can be found in almost any esoteric and occult tradition. The two principles of psychic development are:

- **Work out your mind issues** — your negative habits, bad memories and experiences, worries, concerns, and all your negative emotions that are hidden deep in your subconscious mind. You work them out through meditation, affirmations, core images work, mystical psychotherapy techniques, etc.
- **Improve your overall energetics[2] through energy work** — Yoga, Tai Chi Chuan, Qigong, and New Energy Ways.

A psychic is just a term for a person who perceives more than ordinary people — a person who can receive messages from spirits or read information in energies and perceive energies and spirits. Therefore, we're not really talking about a medium who communicates with those who passed away, or with a person who gives psychic readings by using a crystal ball.

I understand a psychic person as someone who can perceive the deeper reality of things. And I stand by my original thought that turned me into a psychic: everyone has the potential to become psychic, and because of this, everyone has the potential to see things through clairvoyance. All you need is the basic foundation and practice.

---

2 **Energetics** – your energy body, made of energy centers and channels; your spiritual body.

As a basic foundation, we need to understand the principles that I've mentioned above — working with your mind and working with your energetics. This book does not cover these subjects, as it's a book meant for more advanced energy workers who already practice the basics — either from my other books or based on a different tradition (from Wicca to esoteric Buddhism). This book covers the second element, the practice. As such, it contains theory and practical exercises and tips that will teach you everything you need to know about clairvoyance.

Every esoteric or occult path that focuses on the practical aspects, and not just on the theory, is a path that develops both your mind and your energetics. Every magical path includes elements of mind and energy work. That's why both a Buddhist and a Wiccan can learn clairvoyance successfully. The basic principle is practice. If you jump to clairvoyance right away, it might not work. But the more you practice your general esoteric, or magical path, the greater your chances to awakening your inner sight.

So, as long as you stick to the basic foundation of practice and the exercises from this book, then you're on the right path to developing clairvoyance. But how long will it take to start seeing, you may ask. The honest answer is I don't know. My own psychic development took me four years from becoming aware of the possibility to become psychic to actually learning the basics of clairvoyance. And I'm still learning — the learning won't stop. But I know people, as well, who managed to learn clairvoyance within a year, even a few months from starting their practice. So, there's no rule.

As far as I understand this, it all depends on your path, your teachers, the things you learn and practice, and on the mind issues that you need to work out in order to improve your spirituality and energetics. But one thing I know for sure — in the end, everyone can learn clairvoyance. To what degree depends on the person and the amount of practice.

But there's one more thing that you need to understand — it's something rarely anyone talks about these days. You're *already* clairvoyant. You see, as human, you're made of the physical body and spiritual bodies. Since we exist on all these spiritual planes at this very moment, we can perceive these spiritual planes. One of the tricks to do so is to silence the mind, for example, through meditation. But mainly through learning that you can really see things. You already did see them in the past, even if you don't remember it. As kids, we can perceive the spiritual planes. But then, society comes and we are told that what we see isn't real, that we do not have imaginary friends, and that everything is just our imagination. So we block ourselves; as a result, we cannot see anymore. The trick is to reprogram these false beliefs and learn how to see once more.

Those who do not fall victim to socialization remain clairvoyant, and that's how most modern psychics grow — because society failed to persuade them that they can't see while, in reality, they can.

Anyway, let's continue...

Learning the Basics, or the Fast Guy Guide

I understand that this book may be read by people who want to learn clairvoyance but who don't want to learn the basics of psychic development. I understand, also, that most of such people will complain that clairvoyance doesn't work and that this book is a fake. It surprises me that people want to learn how to write a bestselling book without learning to read the alphabet, first...

All right, let's put this sarcasm aside — some people are ready to learn clairvoyance without any previous need for psychic growth. It's natural. Some people are more skilled and gifted than others. But most people *have* to learn the basics, first, before they proceed to learning clairvoyance. It's mandatory. I know, I'm repeating myself, but I wish to make things clear — without the basics, first, you might fail in learning and developing your clairvoyance.

So, if you want to learn clairvoyance, you need to learn a bit about psychic development. You must learn about psychic energies and the life energy that flows within you (Chi, Prana, Ki). You must practice some form of energy work (Chi Kung, Tai Chi Chuan, New Energy Ways, Yoga, etc.). And, once blockages and subconscious patterns begin to re-emerge, you must work with your mind (affirmations, Core Images work, rebirthing, regressing, different forms of meditation). You need to learn basic abilities of grounding, centering, and psychic energy cleansing; you must learn about creating connection with other people as well. This book explains the basic abilities of grounding, centering, and cleansing, along with necessary skills for connecting with objects and people in order to perform a psychic reading, so you don't have to look for them in other books. But this book is not about general psychic development. For this, I refer you to my other book, *Psychic Development Simplified.*

All right — these are the very basics that you need to know. Pretty brief, isn't it? Just remember — if you're not a born-on psychic, and you haven't been born with psychic abilities, then you need to follow some school of psychic development, otherwise learning clairvoyance might be very difficult for you.

Things That You Can See

What can you see through clairvoyance? The world of energies that surrounds us is quite a fascinating place. It is said that everything is energy, and I have to agree. Emotions can be seen as energies; entities are made of energies; we have energies flowing within us, and so on. Before you even start trying to see, you need to learn what you can expect out there. The following list isn't complete. It's because I live in Central Europe, and let's be honest, I might not be familiar with all the energies and entities that can be seen, let's say, in India or South America. While the basic archetypes can be spotted everywhere, I don't think that I know everything.

Because of this, you must keep your "eyes open," as you may see things that I'm not even aware exist. But here are some things that you can perceive clairvoyantly.

Energies in General

Basically, what we see clairvoyantly is energy. What we call "psychic energy" or "spiritual energy" is the same energy, just of different vibrations. Some energies are denser, and they create energetic bodies and entities. Other energies are gentle, and they form Chi (or Prana or Ruach or Ki) — life force. Energies can be seen everywhere — in people, animals, food, rooms, sacred objects, items, or just "in the air." For example, you may look at food to see if it's energized enough to sustain you. Food is the basic source of life energy (Chi); when food lacks energy, then even a big dish can't sustain us.

Energetics of a Place and Objects

Rooms and whole buildings, or even open areas of space, have their own energetics. You can enter a room and use your clairvoyant vision to analyze the energies of the place. (Of course, only if you can't sense the energetics in any other way.) In such a way, I have analyzed the negative electromagnetic fields in rooms in order to know where to put special radionic devices[3] to shield myself from negative energies. In a similar fashion, you can look at different objects, see which of them require energetic cleansing or which of them are very powerful magical objects, too.

Places of power can "shine" nicely, too. I was lucky to see a few such places of power and, I have to admit, the way the energies glow around these places is distinct from everything else around them.

Auras

Living beings have something called an aura around them — a field of energy around the living being. This energy is generated and collected by these beings. Plants, animals, and people have such an aura around them, and you can perceive this aura through clairvoyance. Within the aura, you can see a lot of information about the person, so it's useful if you're thinking about performing psychic readings in the future.

Inner Body Energetics

You can also see deeper into a person and perceive the inner energetics — chakras, energy channels, even inner body organs. As a Reiki practitioner, I use my clairvoyant

---

3 **Radionic devices** – devices and tools made of copper elements and crystals, used to manipulate spiritual energies.

vision to analyze the inner energetics; I see chakras, energy channels (Nadi in Hindu, Meridians in Taoist teachings), and inner organs. I can see what areas of the body lack energy, which chakras require energizing, and what areas of the body need additional Reiki transfer in order to return to a state of harmony. It's quite a useful ability.

Beware! When it comes to analyzing the inner energetics (for example, inner physical organs), remember that as long as you're not a doctor of medicine, you should not make any diagnosis. As a clairvoyant, all you can do is tell the person that some area of the body or specific organ lacks energy, and tell the person to go and see a doctor. It's what I do when I spot problems in the inner energetics.

Psychic Messages

Another category of things that you can perceive by using clairvoyance is messages. In this case, you do not perceive energies directly, but you observe images, scenes, events, movements, and actions. Through this, you can acquire more detailed information, psychic messages, messages from spirits, spirit guides, or even telepathic communication. Our mind thinks through images, not through abstract words. When you think "a horse," you see a horse instead of seeing the word "horse." This is a form of clairvoyance as well. This time, you see complex imagery, and not pure energy.

Spirits

Finally, the last category of clairvoyant vision is the capability to perceive spirits. There are different kinds of spirits that exist on the energetic planes. Below are some examples.

Angels

Angels, as Christianity calls these beings, are a type of spiritual entity that performs different roles in the universe. Some of these entities take care of nature, others act as spirit guides, and so on. They're not necessarily pleasant all the time, and sometimes they may have darker energetics, but they are light beings for sure. In different cultures, Angels have different names, but they're the same type of entities, always.

Deities and Gods

The world is filled with deities from different religions. You shouldn't be surprised at seeing a deity that you used to see only in paintings. Usually, deities can be found in areas where they are worshiped. It's quite possible to perceive, for example, Bodhisattvas from Buddhist traditions. I had such an experience once, and I have to admit that seeing a Bodhisattva is something quite fascinating.

Different cultures have their own pantheons of gods, and gods walk among men. You can see gods by using clairvoyance. I suggest that you ignore them. Show respect, but as long as you're not a faithful believer of a specific religion, don't try to make any deals with gods.

Ghosts

This is a category of spirits usually seen in haunted places or during funerals. A ghost is a remnant of a person — it is said that a ghost is a piece of emotional energy body that might remain on Earth, thus making an earthbound spirit, while the soul goes back to the Source. Anyway, don't play around with ghosts, as they're not as pleasant as some movies teach. Leave it to professionals.

Nature Spirits

These beings can be seen all around us, such as faeries that live in trees, rivers, oceans, and even your house. For example, there are elemental spirits of fire called salamanders. I remember once, when I was a beginner, such a spirit shouted at me when I wanted to put down the candle.

Demons

Demons are a category of spiritual beings from the other side, the dark side — don't be surprised at seeing them, but I hope that you won't see them at all.

Astral Critters

Astral critters (succubi, evil entities, "negs," and so on) can be seen clairvoyantly. These are the lower beings; like animals, they feed on life force, and generally they're not pleasant.

Anyway, these are only some examples of things you can perceive through clairvoyance.

Two Stories, One Lesson

One of my teachers told me a story, passed to him by his friend. The friend was working in a supermarket, and at some point, she decided to "open herself" and look around to see what she could perceive. Not a good idea, as she did see something — a huge, energetic maggot crawling among people, sucking their energies. Not a pleasant view, I imagine. Now you can understand why supermarkets and big box stores have such poor energetics.

Another interesting story comes from a past Halloween, when I decided to take a look at the world outside. It was dark already, and all these shadow entities flowing around gave me the creeps. They were there, flying around as creepy shadows, like ravens seeking their prey.

Why am I mentioning these two events? Well, through clairvoyance, you can see many things. Don't be surprised if you see dark entities or creeping energies — it's normal. And you shouldn't be afraid of this. Also, don't be surprised if you are only able to perceive negative, dark entities clearly, and the energetics of places, objects, or people, but at the same time aren't able to perceive spirit guides or higher spiritual entities. At first, we "tune into" energies of lower vibrations, and it may take time before you are able to see more pleasant energies.

Beware!

Not everything that has wings is an angel or a peaceful nature spirit. Well, even angels can be a pain in the back, if we need some painful lesson. And nature spirits have something we call "ego"; they're not good or bad, they're normal. They may be peaceful or aggressive. If you're sure that what you are seeing is a nature spirit, don't be so sure about its intentions. You might be mistaken.

Demons and negative entities might have wings, too. Some negative entities may even shine like positive, spiritual beings, but they're not. On the other hand, some angels have very dark energetics, and while they're light beings for sure, they may appear to you as dark, even black.

Don't rush towards entities as if they're some kind of peaceful wonder, but gain knowledge and experience first. Only through knowledge and experience will you be able to distinguish between different entities.

Two Types of Seeing

Now we're getting to some secrets. Basically, there are two types of clairvoyance. One is physical and the other is intuitive, or as I used to call it, "inner clairvoyance" or "inner sight." Yes, people can "see" physically; I know quite a few people who can do this. Actually, I have some experience with physical seeing, as well.

Physical Clairvoyance

Physical clairvoyance is quite...physical. I cannot see physically on a daily basis, but I have had two or three experiences of this sort. So I can say that, in the case of physical clairvoyance, you can see things as if they are very, very real — just as you can see the words you read now. Once, when I was young, at age of 16, during my dad's funeral, I saw his spirit standing in the corridor. He looked very real, like a normal person; if I didn't know he was gone, I would be unable to notice any difference between him and all the people around. That was the most intense physical clairvoyance I ever experienced.

Less intense experiences include seeing shadows and lights. Both are quite popular experiences all around the world. They're not really static, more like flashes — you see a shadow or a flash of light (blue or white in my case). It's there for a blink of an eye, and then it's gone — but I could see it physically. I want you to really understand this type of seeing, so here is an example. Have you ever experienced a light bulb blowing up milliseconds after turning on the light? There's a flash of light, and within a blink of an eye, the room is dark again. This is a "large-scale clairvoyant flash." In a similar fashion, other types of energies can be seen physically.

Intuitive Sight, Inner Sight

The second type of clairvoyance is intuitive — it's what I call inner sight. I call it this because it all happens in your head — it's real, but the images you see are shaped in the same area that creates images of your dreams and imagination. There's no eye work included. The images are shaped by your brain, and your brain interprets the psychic messages it receives through something people call "the sixth sense." To understand this better, look below:

Normal Sight
An Eye → Optic nerve → Brain + Perception Filters = Image

Psychic Sight
Psychic Senses (Intuition) → Brain + Filters = Clairvoyance

Inner sight is shown in the second case — through psychic senses, the sixth sense, your brain receives impulses, some kind of information that is later translated into an image. In the same way, the images are shaped through your thoughts, during visualization when you're imagining things or when you experience dreams. The way the images are formed is the same in all these examples; the source of the images, the reason why they appear, is different. That source, this reason, is what I call "psychic intuition" — this is your sixth sense, your psychic sense.

To understand that second type of seeing, this intuitive sight, you can use the following visualization exercises. These exercises will be visualization tutorials at the same time —some time from now you will use visualization as a trigger tool, which will trigger intuitive images. And pay close attention because you're going to learn inner clairvoyance; if you're lucky, from that point you will develop physical clairvoyance, but remember — inner sight is enough and it works quite well. So at first, focus on learning inner sight clairvoyance and allow the physical clairvoyance to develop on its own.

Practicing Visualization

Use the following exercises to learn more about visualization and understand what intuitive clairvoyance looks like.

Exercise 1: Close your eyes and imagine an orange — the fruit. You can "see" it in front of your closed eyes, but it's not realistic. It's blurred, and it seems like it's not there, but this is how visualization works. You imagine something and you visualize it — visualization is a natural ability of the human mind. This is about the quality many clairvoyant images will appear.

Another way of imagining how such inner sight clairvoyance looks is recalling any experience in which you've thought of someone you know, and that person's image appeared in front of your inner mind's eye. Think of a person that you know, and you should already see this person with your mind's eye.

Exercise 2: Think of a horse now. What did you just see in front of your eyes? I think it was a horse, correct? Now, think of a refrigerator — what did you just see in your mind? Think of a tree. Think of an apple. By now, you should already understand the point of this exercise. Our mind does not operate with words but with images. Sometimes, the primary sense is hearing — in that case, a person might be clairaudient. Our brain also thinks with smells and physical feelings. But never with words.

Words are artificial and abstract constructs made by man to improve general communication. There is a theory that before words came into use, prehistoric people were using telepathy to communicate; there's also a theory that animals communicate with telepathy. Personally, I'm far from agreeing with any of these theories, simply because, so far, there is no proof of any of it; but from my personal experience, I can say that we can indeed communicate with others through psychic input and output. But this is a different story; let's get back to clairvoyance.

The second exercise has taught you how clairvoyant images often come to your mind — they just "pop up," appear out of nowhere. The point is to notice them and then interpret them. We will deal with both issues later. For now, know that you have just learned what to expect from basic, intuitive clairvoyance — images appear as visual, and they come out of nowhere.

You can now experiment further with visualization. For example, you can take a book, preferably a novel, and start reading it. Visualize everything that you read — every person, object, and event. Many people do this all the time when they read books; if you haven't done so yet, try it now.

You can also pick up random objects from your environment — notice them, then close your eyes and try to visualize the object.

Both of these simple exercises will improve your visualization — one of the most important elements of clairvoyance.

This book is meant to teach you to use your inner, intuitive sight simply because I do not see physically — at least, not at any given time. In my case, physical clairvoyance happens randomly, maybe once a year. And this is not an experience good enough to write a book about. But don't worry — intuitive clairvoyance is good enough to turn you into a good psychic. The only thing you need to do is to practice, practice, practice... And I guess it's a big secret among psychics. When they teach, they rarely explain to expect *inner* sight to kick in — so people think they should expect physical seeing, which is very rare. Now, if you can only think that you can perceive things through your inner sight, then this whole clairvoyant stuff seems much easier, right?

Third Eye and Intuition

How is it possible that people can see by using clairvoyance? I've explained the theory of different layers of reality, and now it's time for another theory that says that people can *see* because of their Third Eye. The Third Eye is a chakra — the sixth chakra in the system of seven main chakras, according to Theosophical teachings. According to Hindu and Theosophical teachings that build the basics of modern New Age psychic paths, in order to perceive the etherical planes, entities, and energies, you must open your Third Eye. Opening the Third Eye for some people is a form of metaphor, for others it has a literal meaning.

Chakras are energy centers in the human body. Our body is just a physical representation of our being. Invisible to the human eye, there is an energy body. Within it, there are thousands of small chakras and seven main, big chakras. Through these energy centers, life force and our thoughts pass and flow. When the chakra is blocked, the energy cannot flow freely.

For me, opening the Third Eye means cleansing it from negative energies, beliefs, worries, and concerns. You do not "open it," you do not open any chakra, you just cleanse it, you energize it, and you make it work better. When you cleanse the chakra, the energy can flow, at last, and more information reaches your conscious mind. If the chakra is blocked, you experience problems with psychic intuition and clairvoyant seeing.

What is psychic intuition? In her book *Psychic Intuition*, Nancy du Tertre described it quite well. Psychic intuition is a mixture of information picked up by your five primary senses, and probably your sixth sense, as well, which results in you "just knowing what is real." This fact of "knowing," when mixed with a clean and energized Third Eye, creates the foundation for practical clairvoyance. When the Third Eye is clean, the energy can flow, and thus reaches your "intuition center." So the next step is to learn how to listen to, and trust, your intuition.

How do you cleanse your Third Eye? There are many methods. In Appendix A is an article about core images, which is my personal favorite method. For other methods of working out subconscious blockages, you'll need to look around. In this book, I also discuss affirmations, another good method, and further on, I will teach you the Psychonaut Method, as well. And I will also provide you with some tutorials for opening your Third Eye, too. But for now, trusting your intuition is the first thing that we will focus upon.

How to Trust Your Intuition

Learning to trust your intuition is very important. We all experience intuitive thoughts, but we rarely pay attention to this fact. The best way to learn to trust your intuition is to practice intuitive analysis. It's quite a simple thing to do. Whenever you have a decision to make, ask yourself what is the best thing to do — most probably, you will get a lot of answers, lots of options, but one of these options will feel more "right" than others. A lot of options can be very logical and rational, but this one thing, this one option, will feel right from the bottom of your heart. This is the option given to you by your intuition, and in 99% of cases, it's the best thing to do.

The point is to recognize the option "feels right," it's the thing that you *have* to do — it's an emotion, it's a feeling, it's a deeper understanding without any logical or rational basis. If you choose this intuitive option, and it turns out to be the best choice of all, your trust in your intuition will increase. Then, all you have to do is trust your intuitive thoughts more and more. This is how trust is created. There's no better way than that.

You must learn to trust your intuition because clairvoyant images and messages are never logical or rational, but they are intuitive — after all, they are created by your intuitive part of the mind.

About Opening Your Third Eye

There's one more thing that I need to mention in regard to opening the Third Eye. This process must be gentle. You cannot just focus on opening your Third Eye, and Third Eye only. Psychic development is a complex subject, and you must proceed with care. For example, when it comes to opening chakras, you need to open them one by one, starting with the root chakra. Otherwise, you might create new blockages or damage your energy system in such way that you will require help from a professional psychic healer to patch you up.

You should not trust people who offer to open your Third Eye for you — it is not an easy thing to do, but even if it succeeds, you won't be opened to a level you desire. Instead of receiving psychic messages or seeing positive beings, you will see only low vibrations — demons, negative spirits, bad energies, and so on. It's not worth it.

More than that, opening your Third Eye is not enough — you need to walk the psychic path gently because only then will you attune yourself to subtle energies and messages, and only then will you be prepared to work with energies, messages, and entities. Without this, your psychic life will turn into a mess.

Some time ago, I approached a woman working in an ice cream shop. She had a very, very energized and clear Third Eye chakra that caught my attention. I asked her if she can "perceive things" or if she receives any psychic messages. Her answer was negative. This experience proved something I already knew possible from my past chakra readings. Many times I have read people who had their Third Eye wide open, energized, and cleansed of blocking energies, but these people were unable to see clairvoyantly, nor were they able to perform any psychic task.

When you open your Third Eye, you attune yourself to low vibrational energies. With self-growth, development, and practice, you attune yourself to higher and higher vibrations. That's why at first you're beginning to notice your own flaws, fears, and negative energies, and only after many months of practice will you begin to perceive angels, positive spirits, guides, and energies of love. How so?

Opening the Third Eye leads not only to clairvoyance. It gives you an insight into yourself, and into others. Yes, you might be able to look into others and see their worries, concerns, fears, lies, problems, and so on — this can make you a good psychic that will help people with their lives. But remember — you will see into yourself, as well. And you will see bad stuff in yourself, stuff that you will have to deal with in order to develop further on the spiritual path.

Psychic development is directly related to spiritual growth — this cannot be denied. And spiritual growth is not always easy — sometimes, it's very painful because we must face the fears and lies we've hidden deep in our subconscious mind.

These problems, fears, lies, worries, and concerns — every dirt, dust, and stuff that you hide in your subconscious — is called "core images" or "metaprograms." I've written the following description in my other book, *Psychic Development Simplified*:

The term "core images" refers to all negative patterns (beliefs, opinions), memories, and experiences you have. These images not only create blockages, but often they can also act as attachment points for astral entities and psychic vampires, and it's a good idea to remove them in order to get rid of vampiric attachments and astral beings that feed on you.[4]

---

4 *Psychic Development Simplified*, p. 95.

By practicing meditation, or energy work, these core images will be recalled — in most cases, as memories. Sometimes, they might be recalled as feelings or just emotions. As such, they need to be cleansed by using the core images technique, Psychonaut Method, affirmations, or any other technique that deals with elements of the Shadow Self — Zazen meditation is also a nice technique.

Now, I will present an exercise that you can use to trigger a recall of core images so you can work them out later — this is the process of Third Eye cleansing. Be aware — I assume that you have some time of general psychic development behind you and that you know what you're doing. If you haven't practiced psychic development before, do not practice Third Eye opening, it's too dangerous.

Using Meditation and Point Focus to Open the Third Eye

I will teach you how to use basic meditation to help yourself in cleansing your Third Eye. Some people suggest practicing in lotus or half-lotus position (with your legs crossed), but I suggest sitting comfortably, just like that. For example, in an armchair.

When you're sitting, close your eyes and start breathing. Breathe in with your nose, and breathe out with your mouth. Use your diaphragm to breathe. Most people in the West use their upper body to pump the air in and out, but the correct way to breathe is to use your diaphragm — that big muscle in front of your stomach. Breathe without moving your upper body. And breathe gently — there's no need to struggle.

As your breathe, focus on the area of your Third Eye — it's the small area between your eyebrows. You can scratch it with a fingernail to feel it more intensely. The point of this meditation is to focus on that small point. According to a Chinese saying, "energy follows thoughts," so by focusing on your Third Eye, you direct life force into that area. But if you want, you can collect by use of visualization — visualize all energy that is not needed elsewhere to move into your Third Eye, charging it, cleansing and healing it, with each breath in.

Practice this form of meditation for 10 to 15 minutes per day. If you get distracted, don't worry — acknowledge the thought or event and return to focus. Thoughts have a tendency to return when they are chased, so don't chase your thoughts — just relax. Observe the images as they appear, observe the thoughts as they appear. The only thing that concerns you is an image or thought that triggers an emotional response. For example, during the meditation, you may recall a memory that triggers negative emotions — sadness, fear, or similar. This is a core image — write it down in a notebook, as you will have to work it out during a core images session (or any other Shadow Self work).

If no such emotional triggers appear during the meditation, it's okay. You've directed the energy into your Third Eye, and from now on, memories and core images might be recalled in any moment of your life. When they do, work them out. If they don't appear, keep practicing this form of meditation on a daily basis. But remember this simple rule — if you have a core image waiting to be worked out, do not meditate. One core image is enough for now — unless it's worked out, take a break from meditation.

There's a "secret" rarely anyone mentions — most exercises focus on redirecting energy towards the Third Eye. But the truth is, that along with steady and gentle spiritual growth, energy amounts increase a lot, and it finds its way to the Third Eye, anyway. So you have a choice. You can either focus on redirecting the energy to your Third Eye, or you can leave things to themselves, and when you are ready, for real, your Third Eye will be cleansed enough without any effort on your part.

At the end of each session of this exercise, you must ground and center yourself. First do the centering process. Count three index fingers from your belly button down toward your genitals — in your abdomen, there's an energy center called a Tan T'ien. Place both your hands on this area and focus on it. Your focal point should be that small point below your belly button, about two inches inside your body. Focus on this area for two to three minutes, and intend all unnecessary energies to return to this point. Just keep this intention in mind. After two to three minutes, you're done with centering. This exercise will keep your energetics balanced so you won't suffer from the Kundalini Syndrome[5] over time. Remember this centering technique, as you're going to use it almost all the time during the process of psychic work.

Next, ground yourself. For example, visualize energetic roots going from your feet into the ground, and intend all unwanted, dirty energy to leave your body into the ground. Continue this process for two to three minutes. This will get rid of all dirty energies that might have been released during meditation. Grounding is yet another technique that you need to keep in mind.

Continue this exercise (or any other exercise that helps you open your Third Eye), finishing with centering and grounding, for two months before you proceed into practical

---

5 **Kundalini Syndrome** – energetic problem, caused by spiritual growth that is way too fast for spiritual practitioner. It causes emotional and mental inbalance, that leads to mental illness.

clairvoyant work. Until then, keep reading this book, and you will learn a bit more theory.

Opening Your Third Eye with the Use of Crystals and Through Light Energy

If you wish, you can expand the exercise above a bit further. You will need two quartz crystals. Make sure they're properly cleansed. You can cleanse any type of crystal by putting it in salt water for 24 hours, or by burying it in the ground for 24 hours. Then, when the crystals are cleansed, pick up one crystal per hand, so you will have one pure quartz in each hand. Then, close your eyes, and with each breath in, visualize and intend the pure, healing, and positive energy coming from the crystals through your hands into your Third Eye, cleansing and healing it. Continue this exercise for three minutes — no less, no more. And remember to cleanse the crystal after each session of this exercise.

If you wish and if you do not have crystals at hand, then you can use pure, spiritual energy coming from above. Sit down and relax. Then visualize a bright, spiritual energy coming to you from above, flowing into you through the tip of your head, and moving into the Third Eye, cleansing and healing it. Continue this exercise for five minutes, no more.

Opening Your Third Eye with the Use of a Chakra Painting

Another way of opening your Third Eye is through a different form of the first exercise. You need a painting or a picture of the Third-Eye chakra. If you use the power of Google, then you can find such pictures easily — they usually depict a purple Ajna chakra, which contains the symbol of Ohm (Om). It looks like this:

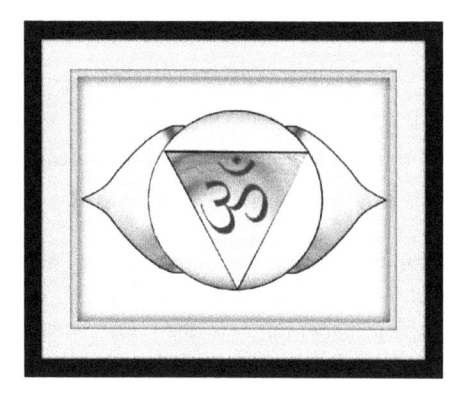

Just place it — even if it's printed on simple computer paper — on the wall, and begin your meditation. Look at the picture of the chakra, and at the same time, focus on your Third-Eye area. Continue this exercise for about 10 minutes, but no more.

In each of these three exercises — crystals, higher energy, painting — remember to bring down the energy back to your Tan T'ien at the end of the exercise. This is an important rule that will keep you safe from the Kundalini syndrome. Also, remember to ground yourself at the end of any of these exercises. These few exercises should be practiced for two months at least. Choose one exercise and stick to it. Choose the one that works best for you and is the easiest one for you.

Finally, remember that such work might bring bad memories and emotions back to you. In such a case, remember to work these memories and emotions out by use of affirmations or core images work, or any other form of spiritual practice meant to deal with negative mind patterns. It's important to do so, as this is the step of healing the Third Eye and opening it further.

Esoteric Safety Rules

Before you proceed further, there are some safety rules that you need to keep in mind if you want to become a real psychic.

- **Do not tune into clairvoyance when you shouldn't** — Too often people "open" themselves (meaning, they turn on their clairvoyant vision) when they shouldn't. In reality, being able to see clairvoyantly is very simple, and it can be turned on "with a switch." When you know how to do this, you just "look" and you can see already. But some places aren't recommended for clairvoyance practice. Some places are filled with negative energies; some places are full of negative entities, and some people just don't like being watched. So either make sure you have very strong psychic defenses or that the place you're tuning in is safe.
- **Do not stare** — People and entities like privacy. When you turn on clairvoyant vision automatically, it's okay. But don't stare too much, especially when your "target" doesn't like it. Some entities and people like to defend their privacy by any means necessary. And in the case of negative entities, when you stare too long, you might attract their attention — this isn't good.
- **Do not be afraid of things you see** — At the same time, do not be afraid of things you see — there's a lot to see, but some energies and entities don't look

nice. You may also see scary messages. Well, don't worry, these are just messages. And in the case of entities, fear might be an invitation. The more you fear, the easier a target you become. So relax and don't be afraid.
- **Ground yourself** — When you use clairvoyance, remember to ground yourself. Visualize energetic roots coming out from your legs into the ground, or eat chocolate, smoke a cigarette, perform any grounding technique so you won't fly away. It's a defensive measure you should remember.
- **Remember to cut yourself off** — Whenever you look at something, whether it's an entity or a person or a place, you create an energetic link, a cord through which energy and thoughts flow in both directions. If you want to stay away from troubles, you must cut the link after every clairvoyant vision. It can be done with simple intention — by thinking to cut yourself off from the target. Or you can visualize a big, energetic sword cutting a visualized link between you and your target.

When you perform any type of psychic work, whether it's simple meditation or a clairvoyant "look," you glow on the energetic plane, and entities can see you. You're like a black fly on a white wall — no matter what you do, those who look at the wall will see you. That's why, along with learning clairvoyance and practicing psychic development, you should learn a lot about psychic self-defense.

Using Affirmations to Set Up a Foundation

Sometimes, problems with clairvoyance originate from wrong beliefs. Some beliefs can be changed through core images work, but sometimes it's best to use affirmations in order to set up a foundation for further work. What is an affirmation?

An affirmation is a phrase that we can repeat constantly, and this repetition is meant to reprogram our mind; for example, we can use affirmations to change our negative habit into a positive habit. [6]

We are being programmed all the time through books we read, movies we watch, lessons in school, from parents at home, and so on. Sometimes we're taught wrong things — false beliefs; in the case of this book, a false belief that clairvoyance isn't real. Because we believe in it on a subconscious level, and the subconscious is a thing through which psychic information must pass, we are being blocked. Affirmations help us reprogram our negative beliefs and program new, positive beliefs.

Now, instead of reinventing the wheel, I will post a longer fragment about affirmations from my other book, *Psychic Development Simplified.* This fragment will be enough to teach you how to work with affirmations.

How to Use Affirmations

A lot of people think that it's sufficient just to repeat an affirmation in your mind in order to get it to work. This isn't

---

6 *Psychic Development Simplified, p. 86*

entirely true. Yes, repeating affirmations in your mind will work, but only if you will repeat it for a few months or even years. A good affirmation should be written down, and it should be written down correctly. What does it mean? Look at the example below, please:

I don't have a headache.

If you repeat this in your mind, then it's an affirmation, but it's a negative affirmation. Why? Because your subconscious mind, upon which we're trying to operate through this technique, doesn't recognize negation. It doesn't understand the word "not" or "no." To your subconscious, the affirmation above looks like this:

I have a headache.

It's as simple as that; your subconscious doesn't care if you want or do not want, if you have or do not have. So when you want to start working with affirmations, you need to pay attention now, as there are a few things you need to learn first.

How to Create Good Affirmations

First of all, a good affirmation must keep you thinking in a positive way. It cannot include any negative words or phrases. Below are a few examples of bad affirmations:

I don't have a headache.
I'm not worried.

Instead, you should create affirmations that say "my head feels good and okay," "I'm calm and secure." An affirmation must be always positive in order to replace any negative pattern you might have stored in your subconscious mind. Below are more examples of good affirmations:

I, Nathan, am happy.

I, Nathan, am innocent (if someone is accusing you).

I, Nathan, work efficiently and I like my job (if you have problems in the workplace).

I, Nathan, experience pleasure each and every day.

I, Nathan, have the right to feel safe in my home (if you feel threatened).

Quite simple, isn't it? Generally, as I've stated earlier, we create negative patterns throughout our entire life. Emotional traumas, scary events, bad experiences — they all create our behavior habits, and some of the habits we just can't stand. Affirmations are one of the methods to reprogram our mind and change negative habits and negative thoughts into positive habits and positive thoughts.

Notice there's always "I, NAME, something" — it's an affirmation for you, so it should include your name. Remember, it's a tool to work with your subconscious, and your subconscious needs a name for identification. Just stick to this rule.

Let's say you're always tired at work, but you do like your work; you do what you love, yet you don't experience that energy burst some people have. You might figure out it's because a few years earlier, you were working in a place you didn't like, and you lost your interest in any kind of work. This is a negative habit. You can now use affirmation to reprogram your mind. Simply by focusing on "I'm always full of energy during work," you can become a walking power cell once more.

An interesting fact is that affirmations are tools to work with your subconscious, and your subconscious is a nasty pet. For example, if you change that affirmation a little into "I'm always full of energy in my workplace," then it will work as well. But notice the keyword "workplace." Now what might happen if your boss sends you with a delegation? You're no longer in your workplace, and your energy might decide to take a break. Remember to pay close attention to your keywords.

As I said, affirmations are tools to work with your subconscious. If you focus on each affirmation, and you focus on it with your heart and brain, after a few days, perhaps a few weeks or months, it starts to overwrite your previous subconscious pattern. It's like a mechanical way to deal with these subconscious problems. Personally, I use affirmations to deal with problems I cannot identify as core images, as I can't work with them with my standard practice.

The best way to explain how affirmations really work will be to give you simple examples from my own practice. I had problems with money. I wanted to make more money from my own businesses, but I was just unable to. Some inner growth practices have pointed me to the source of the problem. I had that negative pattern in my mind that was constantly telling me two things:

- **First, something that others have taught me in the past** — that it's hard to earn money.
- **Second, something I had taught myself** — that those who are rich are dishonest assholes.

So I had to deal with these negative patterns. The first one was telling me that I can't really make money easily and with pleasure. The second one was even more problematic.

How could I become rich if I consider everyone who is rich to be an asshole? Well, I've created two affirmations: "I, Nathan, make money easily and with pleasure" and "I, Nathan, have great respect for people who honestly achieved success." Within less than two weeks, I managed to deal with both negative patterns.

My income jumped about 30%, and I've gained inspiration for dozens of articles and four more new e-books I will write this year. That's for the first affirmation. For the second one, here's an example. My friend, Courtney, published an article in the latest *TAPS Paramagazine* issue. Normally, I would envy her and even feel sad because she did it and I didn't. But honestly, when I learned about her success, I was as happy as if it were me who got published. An awesome change of viewpoint!

You see how affirmations work. Earlier, I said that affirmations might work after a few days, weeks, or even months. Indeed, there's no set-in-stone time for affirmations because some negative patterns in your mind are weaker than others, and some are more established than others. Weak patterns can be dealt with in a few weeks, and difficult and established patterns might require a few months to overwrite. How to know when an affirmation starts working? To understand this, you need to learn how to write and use affirmations.

How to Write and Use Affirmations

Before I explain how to write affirmations, I want to say that there are other methods of using affirmations, as well. You can record them and listen to them with your mp3 player; you can speak them aloud a few times a day; you can paint them; you can type them on a computer. However, based on the experience of many people, you should know that these methods require a lot more time for an affirmation to work. The best way, in my opinion, is through handwriting.

Therefore, you need a notebook. You shouldn't use the same notebook that you're using as your psychic journal. Use a new, fresh notebook and devote it solely for the purpose of affirmations. When you open it, you can write your affirmations on the left page. On the right page, you should write all your responses. What is a response in the case of affirmations? When you write an affirmation, you get a response from your body — it's either a physical response or an emotional or mental one. For example, you might:

Feel physical pain, recall past memories, feel emotional pain, or fear, or get any kind of emotion — positive or negative. You might even have positive physical responses, like pleasure, or you can get simple thoughts like "this is not real," "this is stupid," or "this is fake." You may get positive thoughts like "awesome," "yeah, it's true." All these responses should be written down with no judgment — just write them, and don't judge yourself because you have some negative thoughts. If you focus on them, you might get angry or scared, and this only makes things worse.

The point is to write all these responses on the right page so they won't be stuck in your subconscious anymore. An affirmation starts working when you get only positive responses from your body and mind; it means when you write your affirmations, you get only positive sensations, thoughts, and emotions, with no negative responses. This might take weeks or even months.

Some schools of thought say that you should write affirmations for 30 days, or even for 90 days. Well, my school of thought is different. You should write down affirmations for seven days at least — if after seven days you still get negative responses, then continue writing your affirmations until you get positive responses only. This is the only rule you should stick to when it comes to answering the question "how long should I write?" Personally, today I write affirmations for no less than 21 days — but usually, I expand this period to 30 or even 40 days.

So how should you write affirmations, anyway? You already know they should be as positive as possible. But you can't just write "I'm happy" because the way we perceive ourselves is not just our view. I mean, the way you see yourself is shaped by your thoughts and the thoughts, opinions, and gossip of other people. Therefore, you should write down each affirmation from three perspectives, like this:

I, Nathan, make money simply and with pleasure.
You, Nathan, make money simply and with pleasure.
He, Nathan, makes money simply and with pleasure.

And this set of affirmations should be repeated five times, so in total, you will write 15 phrases. If you're dealing with a difficult pattern, you can also write 30 phrases or even more, if you like. As you can see, writing affirmations is quite simple.

Working with Affirmations

When you write affirmations, please don't act like a machine — feel real enjoyment when you write each word, use your heart and "love" the phrases you're writing. By adding positive emotions to positive affirmations, you're improving their effects; they just work better. But if you write things down automatically just to write them, then they won't really work as they should be. So, feel positive!

I need to mention a very important thing. After a few days or perhaps weeks of writing your affirmations, you might experience a mental breakdown. You may get sad, angry, and you may think this doesn't work. Do not stop writing affirmations now because such a breakdown is a sign that the affirmation is beginning to overwrite your old patterns! You must be strong because a few days later negativity will be gone, and your affirmation will really start to work. Some people experience these breakdowns and some don't. But if you experience it, remember to keep writing affirmations, as such emotional breakdowns are a good sign.

Affirmations to Improve Clairvoyance

The instructions above should help you learn how to write good affirmations. When you do know how to write affirmations, and how to work with them for best benefits, I can give you some examples of affirmations to experiment with, meant to directly improve your clairvoyant abilities. Consider these affirmations as a foundation; they might not awaken your clairvoyant ability, but they might reprogram your mind to such a degree that learning clairvoyance will be a lot easier.

I, NAME, allow myself to perceive the energies and entities around me.
I, NAME, am capable of perceiving energies and entities around me with my inner sight.

I, NAME, allow myself, and I'm able to perceive, psychic messages via my inner sight.

I, NAME, can perceive auras and a person's energies via my inner sight.

I, NAME, am allowed to use clairvoyance.

I, NAME, understand that clairvoyance is my natural ability.

I, NAME, understand that clairvoyance is real.

I, NAME, recognize clairvoyance as an ability that I can learn.

I, NAME, trust my intuition.

I, NAME, allow the universe to guide me in improving my clairvoyance.

The affirmations above, when practiced properly, will help you build a foundation for your future clairvoyant work. Of course, it will take many months to work these affirmations out, but it's worth it. Remember — when you get a response from your subconscious, write it down and create your own affirmation. Also, think about clairvoyance — think about your beliefs about clairvoyance, your blockages, and programs that you may store in your subconscious, and create new affirmations that you can use. You can work with affirmations along with exercises that open your Third Eye.

Please note — knowledge of affirmations can be used in any field of your life — love, money, passion, etc. Don't hesitate to use them in other areas of your life.

The Basic Understanding

So, here's the basic drill: practice a technique of cleansing and healing your Third Eye. Whenever any negative emotions, bad memories, bad beliefs about clairvoyance, or any negative mind pattern re-emerges from your subconscious mind — heal it! Use affirmations, core images (for which I'm offering guided meditation and tutorials on the *A State of Mind* website), or simple Zazen meditation and such, and heal the pattern. Then, go back to the practice of healing your Third Eye. After two months, you will be able to move further into a more practical clairvoyance practice. It's quite simple, isn't it?

Preparing Your Room, Preparing Yourself

While you practice affirmations each day, you should learn a bit about the environment that you're going to practice clairvoyance in. In most cases, you will be practicing in a private room. Such place should be prepared for any form of psychic work to make it safe for you to work. After all, during the opening process for receiving information, you allow different energies to enter your energetic body. It's wise to keep your environment clean and safe so you can practice safely.

For this purpose, you should learn how to create your sacred space. A sacred space is a room dedicated for spiritual and psychic work. Dedicated means that you do not do anything but spiritual and psychic work in such a room. This way, you keep it energetically balanced and clean. As a result, such a place improves your overall psychic and spiritual training.

How to Create Sacred Space

Now that you know what sacred space is and why you should use it, you can learn how to create it. First of all, you need to choose the room — it might be an attic or basement, or a normal room in your house that is not used at all. Or it can be a house placed deeply in the forest, or a mountain cabin, a place that looks like a temple, or a room with naked brick — whatever! The choice is yours, what really matters is that the place needs to be quiet and not disturbed by anyone, as you already know.

Then, you should follow these steps.

1. **Clean the room** — You need to clean the room of all items, objects, and garbage of any sort. Leave no furniture, no artificial lights, nothing at all. The place must be cleaned totally. This is the first thing to do, and the most physical thing to do.
2. **Cleanse the room** — Then you need to cleanse the room of negative energies. If you're an energy worker, you can use energy manipulation skills and scrub the walls of energies, throwing them away. Here's a simple tutorial to do so. First, sit down inside the room and visualize all negative, dark energies being thrown through doors or through the window — just visualize it, or in other words, imagine it. Then, visualize bright white light covering the entire room; try to feel a light breeze inside it. These are semi-magical, or should I say, semi-psychical (psychic) steps to make. After this, take a candle, place it in a pot, and place the pot inside the room. Sprinkle salt around the place and light the candle. Let it burn out (it might take some time). Then light incense (of any sort, you might want to consult some books or websites to choose the best, but in my eyes, any natural incense will do the trick); let the incense burn out as well. Candle heat, salt, and incense smoke are known for their

cleansing capabilities, and yes — this is magical work right now. Finally, if you have wind bells, you can hover the inside the room and open all doors and windows, and air the room. This will cleanse the room of all negative energies and prepare it for magical purposes.
3. **Decorate the room** — Some people prefer their sacred space to be spartan in look — no fabric, no furniture, nothing at all. Others like to decorate the room — attach some fabric to the walls, add some candles, and so on. I suggest that you should not get the room too dirty. It should remain as simple as possible. But, definitely, a piece of fabric should be placed on all windows, and it should cover the doors, as well. The room must be dark, as light tends to disrupt proper magical energies. The best advice I can give you here is that the room should have a nice feel to your eyes; if you're thinking about an extremely Gothic-like room like the one in old vampire movies, go for it! Just make sure the room won't get cluttered.
4. **Ward the room** — Finally, if you're an energy worker, you can also ward the room. A ward is created through visualization. You can visualize an energetic shield around the room and intend it to block all unwanted or negative energies. Remember to recharge the ward from time to time. Sit down and with closed eyes visualize bright white light covering all walls, windows, doors, floor, and ceiling of the room. Visualize this bright white light becoming a solid mass that cannot be passed by any other energies. That's it — the room is now warded.

And now you are done — you have created your sacred space. Nobody should be allowed in your sacred space, as they will disrupt the energies. The more spiritual and psychic work you perform there, the stronger the energy will become. Never get angry in your sacred space — let it remain sacred and peaceful. If you're angry or afraid, get outside or find another room. No negative energies should be allowed in your sacred space.

The creation process of your sacred space might take two days or a whole week — that depends on how much garbage you have in the room. If you still feel some residual energies inside it after cleansing, use candles and incense again.

Of course, the above is a place intentionally prepared for training purposes. But you may need to open your inner sight in places where such preparations are impossible. You can do this — but only after you feel you're ready, meaning, when you feel you have learned enough about psychic self-defense.

How to Protect Yourself

Preparing a training room is one thing. Learning how to protect yourself is another. First, you should learn how to create a psychic shield — a basic defensive measure. This is taught in most psychic workshops, and in most psychic development books, as well. Again, there's no need to reinvent the wheel, so here's a tutorial I've published in the past.

How to Create a Psychic Shield in Six Steps

- **Center** — centering is the process of clearing and focusing your mind. Just focus your mind on the middle of you. This simple process brings you to the "here and now," and it is called "centering." That middle point is your lower Tan T'ien — an area in your abdomen, which I already have mentioned. Just focus on your lower Tan T'ien, and you're centered.
- **Set your intention** — decide what you want. You want to create a psychic shield that will block any negative and unwanted energies from entering you. Keep the intention in your mind.
- **Set up the shield** — now feel the energy (using your favorite energy manipulation system, for example, basic visualization) leaving your inner body and forming either a bubble around your body or an additional layer to your skin. Keep the previous intention inside your mind at all times.
- **Shell** — when the shield is up, it's time to shell it. Feel or visualize it becoming hard, impenetrable (this process is called shelling), and after you're done, you're done. The shield is up. And it's your basic psychic self-defense measure.

How to Lower the Shield

When the shield isn't needed anymore, it should be "lowered"; this means it should be destroyed. This is very simple: have an intention to lower the shield, then feel or visualize it disappearing while keeping the intention of lowering it in your mind. As you can see, both setting up and lowering the shield is very easy, and in most cases, it's possible to achieve success the first time you try it. Remember, it's all about the intention and energy manipulation, and we all know that energy follows thoughts.

Tips for Remaining Safe

No matter whether you do your psychic work in your sacred space, or if you work "in the field," you should remember a few safety tips.

- **Light a candle** — no matter where you are, when you perform a psychic reading or any form of clairvoyance, if there's such a possibility, light a candle. Fire is a well-known means to keeping the area safe of negative energies. Candles are your friend, really! They contain elemental spirits that burn negative energies. Remember to let the candle burn itself out; do not try to put it down yourself unless you really have to, for example, due to a fire hazard.
- **Ground yourself** — grounding is a process of connecting yourself with the Earth. Often, when people perform spiritual or psychic work, such as clairvoyance, they tend to "fly away." They might lose their grounding, enter altered states of consciousness, become lost in psychic messages and images, or even become prey for astral critters. Grounding is a safety measure that keeps you anchored to the ground and allows you to return from your "spiritual trip." Grounding can be performed through visualization — you can visualize energy roots extending from your legs into the ground, grounding you. If this won't help, you can eat something sweet — for example,

chocolate. Sweet food is a good grounding measure. Smoking a cigarette or a pipe is also a great way to ground yourself.
- **Center** — centering should be performed along with grounding. As I said earlier, it's quite simple: focus on your Tan T'ien.
- **Cleanse** — when you do clairvoyance, you collect energetic dust, especially when you do psychic readings; you collect energies from people you read. After each reading, you should cleanse yourself. You can take a bath in salt water. If you do not have a bath, rub salt on your body under the shower. You can also light incense and stand above it for a few minutes, allowing the smoke to cleanse you. These are the simplest methods of cleansing yourself.
- **Do not panic!** — sometimes, your clairvoyance might "turn on" on its own, and you might start to see things when you don't want to. In such a case, do not panic. Ground yourself, center yourself, and feel no fear.

Finally, a few more words about cleansing. Remember to cleanse yourself of negative energies regularly — if you can, do this every single day. It's because we collect unpleasant energies on our aura all the time, and if you wish to remain spiritually safe, then spiritual and psychic cleansing is mandatory. Also, remember that if you collect too many negative energies on your aura, then your abilities to perform clairvoyance will get weaker, and you might become "blind" entirely until you cleanse yourself. I will teach you more about cleansing negative energies from your aura in just a few pages.

With these simple tips, you will remain a safe clairvoyant — at least, to some degree. In the field of psychic phenomena, you can never be sure what might happen, so you must be ready for everything.

The Alpha State

You practice meditation, you've prepared a room to practice in, and you've learned about safety rules — it might be boring, but without these skills, you won't be able to safely practice and use clairvoyance. Now, it's time to learn about the alpha state. The alpha state is a state of mind in which your brainwaves oscillate in the frequency range of 8–12 Hz. In simple words, this is the state in which your body is relaxed and your mind is calm. The deeper the state, the more relaxed your body is. And this is the state of mind in which clairvoyance occurs. That is why your next step in learning clairvoyance is learning how to enter the alpha state of mind.

You should already know this if you have ever practiced meditation or any technique of relaxation. Months of experience in meditation allows your mind to relax very, very fast — in a matter of seconds. Lot of experience in meditation should allow you to enter the alpha state very quickly. But if you do not have experience in meditation or any form of relaxation, then you need to learn it. There are many methods to choose from — different forms of meditation are easily available. Personally, I recommend Silva's method of mind control, or The Gateway Experience. Both methods are very effective and can teach you how to enter the alpha state quickly.

But if you do not have access to any meditation workshop, or you cannot afford such course on CDs, then don't worry. I have a simple yet time-consuming technique for you. Like all techniques of this kind, it is based on programming your mind. In other words, you need to teach your mind how to relax quickly on your conscious signal. Follow these steps:

- **Sit down comfortably in an armchair.** I do not recommend a bed because you want to remain conscious, and people have a tendency to fall asleep when they lie down. So sit down and close your eyes.
- **Calm your breath**. Relax and breathe normally.
- **Start counting down from 100 to 1.** Count slowly, take a breath in, say the number in your mind, and slowly breathe out. Then breathe in again, and say another number. When you reach number one, you will be in the alpha state. When you do this, say to yourself, in your mind, "I've reached number one. I'm now in alpha state. My mind is calm but awake, and my body is deeply relaxed, almost asleep."
- **Spend a few minutes repeating this phrase in your mind.** Then count up, from one to five, and when you reach number five, say to yourself, "I've reached number five, I'm fully awake now." Then open your eyes.
- When you get lost, for example because of some thoughts or because of falling asleep, you need to start counting again.

That's it — you've reached alpha state, and you've returned to the normal world! But you don't want to count down from 100 to 1 each time you need to find yourself in alpha state. That's why this simple exercise is turned into an entire training program. Practice the above exercise each day, seven days a week. Each week, decrease the start number — for example, from 100 to 90, from 90 to 80 and so on. Look at the table below for references.

Week 1	100 to 1
Week 2	90 to 1
Week 3	80 to 1
Week 4	70 to 1
Week 5	60 to 1
Week 6	50 to 1
Week 7	40 to 1
Week 8	30 to 1
Week 9	20 to 1
Week 10	10 to 1

You need to perform each "start number" seven days in a row without interruption (without getting lost in the count and without falling asleep). With time and practice, you will reach number ten as your start number. From that moment on, you will be able to enter the alpha state simply by counting down from ten to one. Then you will be ready for some serious clairvoyance.

If any thoughts reach your mind during the countdown, let them be. Acknowledge them and return to counting. When you chase your thoughts, they tend to return. If you do not chase them, at some point they simply disappear. This exercise has one more purpose — it will help you relax. In the modern world, with people so stressed, it's another benefit from learning clairvoyance.

After a few months, you will have a great tool to work with — not only for clairvoyance, but also for relaxation and many other things. To a mind that is still, the whole universe surrenders, as Lao Tsu used to say.

Focusing on the Third Eye

Energy follows thoughts, as you should know already. And the Third-Eye chakra requires fuel to operate. Once in the alpha state, you might want to charge up your Third-Eye chakra a bit. You can do this in multiple ways, for example, through focus or through visualization. First, through focus: simply focus on the area of your Third Eye for a minute or two — with time, you might require no more than a few seconds for the Third Eye to become charged. If you can't "feel" the Third-Eye chakra, scratch the area between your eyebrows, and it should help you out.

If you want, you can use visualization for the process of charge-up. Simply visualize the energy flowing from your lower Tan T'ien area, below your belly button, into the Third Eye, charging it with psychic life energies.

Remember to ground yourself and direct the energy into the lower Tan T'ien after each clairvoyant session — this is a safety rule you *must* obey.

Psychic Energy Cleansing

Before we proceed further, I wish to teach you a bit about energy cleansing, since rarely do modern New Age books mention this subject. When you look around through clairvoyance, you open yourself, and the more open you are, the more negative energies you collect upon your own aura.

This happens during psychic readings for others, as well, or during psychometry and other forms of psychic work. It is important to know how to cleanse yourself and keep your aura clean.

The simplest way is to light a candle and use your hands to collect energies from your aura, and cast them into the flame. Just use your hands to grab the energies and cast them — from your torso, hands, legs, back, and head. Energy follows thoughts, so if you keep an intention of collecting negative, dirty energies from your aura, the energies will be collected. Then cast them into the flame, and when you're done, cut the link between you and the flame. Allow the candle flame to burn out on its own.

Or, you can light incense on the floor — any type of natural powder incense will work, and if you have access to white sage, then it will work nicely, as well. Then stand above the incense and allow the smoke to cover you from the bottom to the tip of your head. Smoke generated by natural incense has cleansing capabilities, and it is often used in different forms of cleansing work, for example, cleansing magical rituals. Stand in the smoke for five minutes, and your aura should be cleansed.

You can also use salt. Natural salt works best, but you can use kitchen salt. If you have a bath, then add a bit of salt to water — let's say three or four spoons. Then take a normal bath, and the salt will cleanse your aura. If you do not have a bath but a shower, you can rub salt into your entire body with the intention of energetic cleansing, and then wash the salt off with water. It will work in the same way. Salt is known for its cleansing capabilities.

These are the simplest methods that can be used by everyone, as salt, candles, and natural incense are easily available, and they're easy to use. Practice such cleansing at least once a week, and after every form of spiritual work or practice. And if you offer psychic services, then cleanse yourself with smoke or candle and energy work between each customer. This will keep your aura clean and healthy.

Summary

You have learned that there are two types of clairvoyance and that you're going to learn how to use the second type, the inner sight, which is enough for you to work with clairvoyance effectively. You've learned some safety rules, meditation techniques, and exercises that will help you open your Third Eye. You also have learned that through your practice, you might experience negative thoughts, bad memories from the past, negative beliefs and such — these are core images. And you have learned how to work them out — through affirmations and core images. Finally, you have learned how to protect yourself and how to create a sacred space in which you're going to practice clairvoyance at first. Now, with all this knowledge and with months of experience that you have in general psychic development, you can proceed to the book of practice, which will teach you practical exercises that will help you learn and develop clairvoyance.

The Book of Practice

All right, the worst is behind you. I know people don't like theory! From now on, theory will be kept to a minimum, and I will focus on practical aspects of clairvoyance. You will learn how to use the Psychonaut Method for personal self-growth and further improvement of clairvoyance, and you will learn about psychic readings, auras, chakra reading, and more. We will start with the clairvoyant laboratory — a technique that is quite useful for spiritual growth and psychic readings.

The Clairvoyant Laboratory Technique

As always, you should start with the basics. The clairvoyant laboratory technique is a basic method that will introduce you to more complex work, and in the future, it can be used for psychic readings if you want. Often, clairvoyant psychics say that in order to acquire information, they need to visit their private sacred space. It is an area within their mind, a place where they can pick up psychic data and interpret it. But rarely does any psychic explain what this sacred space is or how it works. I'm going to share my sacred space with you now, and reveal the secret:

I close my eyes, take a few deep breaths, and relax. Then, I visualize myself standing in the center of a large library. This is my sacred space for psychic work.

This mental sacred space is my clairvoyant laboratory. It has been visualized by me and programmed to exist within my mind. It's quite simple. It's a visualized area, or even a wall upon which pictures appear. It is all about visualization and letting go of your conscious control over the images. Within such visualized space within your mind, you can pick up psychic data in various ways — through sounds, smells, images, and feelings. But mainly through images.

Within my personal library, there are bookshelves, and I can pick up and open every single book. There are doors that I can open. There are pictures on the walls and desks to sit by. There are many objects I can interact with. When I need to know something, I let go of the control of my visualization. I see the library, and I follow my intuition. It guides me to the bookshelf in the right corner of the library. I pick up the book that I sense I should pick up. And I open it, and I look at it without any control over the images. But the images appear, and all I have to do is interpret them. Then, I have my psychic answer. This is the clairvoyant laboratory that I use for my psychic practice. And this is the famous sacred space all these psychics talk about.

Another example of a psychic sacred space, a clairvoyant laboratory, comes from the teachings of Debra Katz. For her own clairvoyance, she used to visualize a large black screen in front of her eyes, upon which pictures and messages could appear. You can try it, as well — whether it's a cinema screen, or a modern TV, or a theater scene — it's your choice. It will work — why? Well...

Why Does the Clairvoyant Laboratory Work?

Your subconscious mind has troubles with throwing random images on a "blank screen." Often, it just cannot give you images if there isn't any anchor point to attach them to. This won't be a problem later on when your automatic clairvoyance kicks in, but at first, you will need a focal point — a hook or an anchor point. A clairvoyant laboratory is such an anchor point. In other words, if psychic information you've picked up does not have a "hook," it might not be displayed to you in any form. In the case of clairvoyance, the hooks are images that you visualize. When they're visualized, and you have an intention to acquire specific information, then all you have to do is to let go of the illusion of control, and observe. If there are any impressions or messages coming through your psychic senses, they will hook themselves, and you will be able to perceive them consciously.

It's exactly what I do when I "pick up a random book" in my visualized library. I visualize. I keep an intention, and then, I let go. If there is a message or information for me to pick up, I will pick it up, so I can pass it to my client, for example.

The clairvoyant laboratory can be expanded into other forms of psychic perception. As I said, psychic information needs to have a hook to attach itself to it, and become a conscious thought that you can perceive. I'm clairvoyant, so I attach psychic impressions to images.

How to Create a Clairvoyant Laboratory

As you should know already, creating your clairvoyant laboratory is all about visualization. You need to visualize yourself a place in which you will be performing your psychic work. So, sit down for a while and close your eyes.

- Take a few deep breaths and relax. Enter an alpha state with your favorite method. See the darkness in front of your eyes.
- Think about what kind of space you want to create for yourself. Is it a library? Or maybe your home? A large Victorian mansion? Or maybe a scientific lab? Visualize a space that you enjoy. You need to like the place in which you work. It's a psychological thing.
- Fill the place with interactive objects. For example, add bookshelves; a desk; a plant; a few doors; a computer; a large LCD screen. The point is to have as many objects to interact with as possible. Think about what else you can add to your laboratory.
- Finally, when everything is in place, memorize the place. You're going to return here soon. That's it. You've prepared yourself your very own clairvoyant laboratory. And any time you want to return there, the place should be the same. Any differences carry a message, so pay attention to things that change within your clairvoyant laboratory.

I've mentioned a large Victorian mansion. I've a word of advice here because some of you might want to create a haunted building for your psychic work. With such visualization, you add an intention for the building to be haunted, and you expect it to be haunted. Thus, you might accidentally attract spirits, ghosts, and even negative entities to your life. Please, don't do this. Spirit communication and dealing with ghosts are very advanced skills, and slightly dangerous things to do; I don't recommend it.

So, don't intend for your sacred space to be haunted because you might get what you wish for when you're not ready for this.

How to Enter and Leave Your Clairvoyant Laboratory

In order to enter your clairvoyant laboratory, you need to take a few deep breaths and relax. Clear your mind and chill out. Enter the alpha state. Then, simply visualize the laboratory you've created. See the objects, the walls, all the doors, etc. In order to leave the laboratory, all you have to do is open your eyes and become conscious of your physical world once again. You might want to add grounding and centering skills to your work with the laboratory. As you can see, it's very simple.

How to Use Your Clairvoyant Laboratory

In order to explain how to use your lab, we need an example situation. Let's assume that you're doing a psychic reading for someone. So a client, let's call him Joe, asks, "What is the source of my financial problems?" You need to enter your clairvoyant laboratory, and with this intention in your mind, answer the question.

- Relax, enter an alpha state of mind. Enter the lab by closing your eyes and visualizing yourself standing in your psychic space.
- Ask the question: "What is the source of financial problems for Joe?" Start hunting for information and messages. Relax and clear your mind; notice if you're attracted to any object in your sacred space. Let go of control and follow your intuition (it will develop with time and practice of the basic psychic awakening exercises).
- You might be attracted to a room you have never seen before, and see a person there. Ask the person its name. Let's say a person's name is Emily. So ask your client if he knows someone called Emily. Maybe she's his ex-wife who took all his money during a divorce. He may be attached to this fact and he can't let it go, so he attracts more financial problems.
- Or you might be attracted to a book. Open it and see what's inside. Maybe there is a photo of a car. And maybe Joe has bought a new car, but in order to do so, he decided to live in debt. Or the book might be empty, which can be interpreted not as "there's no answer to your question, Joe," but as "you have no plans for the future, you're empty, you need to set yourself some goals." Interpretation can be tricky.
- When the answer is provided, you can leave your lab and wait for another question or end the reading. Don't forget to break the link with your client when you're done, and with all the objects you've read.

I think this should give you the basic idea of how your clairvoyant laboratory works. It's very simple — you visualize the lab, you set the intention, and then you let go. All you have to do next is interpret what you perceive.

Additional Tips

You can continue to organize your sacred psychic space. For example, you might intend for things related to the past to appear on the right, and things related to the future to appear on the left, while the things related to the present will appear in the middle of your sight. To program your lab in such a way, all you have to do is keep that intention every time you practice in your lab.

When you cannot see anything, there may be a few reasons for this. For example, you might need to interpret the empty message. Or it might mean that your intuition isn't developed enough and you need to spend more time with the basics before you can practice advanced stuff.

The clairvoyant laboratory technique is a great way to improve your results in clairvoyance. And it can be used for psychic healing (when performing a diagnosis), in chakra reading, in psychic reading, and in psychometry practice. It's a useful tool to work with, but as with everything, it takes time to master. At first, you might have trouble with visualization and with following your intuition. But keep practicing, and with time, you will get better and better. Psychic abilities are no different from learning any other skill, from riding a bike to drawing and programming.

Remember, this advanced technique might not work if you haven't finished your basic psychic development practices, such as energy work, mind re-programming, etc. People tend to jump to advanced stuff right away, and then they're sad if nothing works for them. Please, don't do this — the basics are fascinating, and they can lead to really fast results. And the best part is — when you're done with the basics, then the advanced things shall hold no secrets. The clairvoyant laboratory is a basic of clairvoyance, but an advanced technique on the general psychic development path.

You can use this laboratory to work with your own intuition in every aspect of your life. For example, if you're thinking about a new business, you can enter the laboratory and ask a personal question regarding the new business, and follow the intuitive messages that appear through feelings and clairvoyant images. Businesses, relationships, friends, love, family, work — you can use the clairvoyant laboratory and your own intuition in every single area of your life. Later on, you will learn how to use the lab for spiritual journeys and spiritual development, as well.

The clairvoyant laboratory technique will be expanded upon over the next pages. You will learn how to use this technique for spiritual journeys and for observing energies, entities, and people. I will guide you through some uses, and other ways to use the lab I will leave to you. You will figure out additional ways to use this technique, I'm sure of it.

The Psychonaut Method — A Spiritual Journey

Now that you have learned how to use the simple technique of a clairvoyant laboratory, we're going to use it and help you with your own spiritual growth. You might ask, "Why do I need to deal with spiritual growth? I just want to learn clairvoyance!" Well, that's what we're going to do. First, spiritual growth is important for clairvoyant development. The more spiritual you are, the better your clairvoyance is. But don't worry — spirituality isn't about sitting in a temple for 24/7 or becoming a monk. It's about learning how to live a peaceful and happy life. For those interested in grounded spirituality, I recommend my other book, *Living with Reiki.*

Anyway, the Psychonaut Method will teach you two things. First, it will allow you to identify more blockages and negative mind patterns that will help you improve your life. Secondly, through practice of this spiritual journey technique, you will open your Third Eye further and improve your intuition. Through observation of your inner self, your subconscious mind, you improve your clairvoyant vision — a form of vision that does not simply let you see spirits, but also allows you to receive psychic and spiritual messages. And the more you perceive this way, the more open your Third Eye gets, and the better your communication with intuitive mind is. And this, of course, will benefit your general psychic and clairvoyant growth.

Now, a word of warning: the spiritual journey of the Psychonaut Method might be painful, as any form of true spiritual path is. You might see the dark side of your own soul, or you might recall bad memories from the past. Don't worry — these things won't harm you anymore. But recalling them, becoming aware of them, helps you realize your true nature and heal negative emotions. The more negative emotions you heal (fears, for example), the better your life becomes. Don't worry; be strong and practice.

This technique is a mixture of core images work along with the Rabbits Hole technique developed by Agnieszka Cupak.

How to Use the Psychonaut Method

You're going to use the clairvoyant laboratory technique for this spiritual journey. First, just sit down and relax. Close your eyes and enter the alpha state — as always in case of clairvoyant laboratory. I'm going to teach you two versions of this method, one that includes only you and another one that include the support from your spirit guide. Basically, we all have at least one spirit guide at our side, and if we want, a spirit guide can help us in our spiritual growth. If you do believe in spirit guides, then ask the guide to help you with the Psychonaut Method. If you do not believe in spirit guides, just skip the "ask the guide for help" point.

1. **Enter your clairvoyant laboratory** — sit down, relax, enter the alpha state, and see the lab you've created.
2. **Set an intention to heal some part of you**. Ask yourself what kind of problems you have right now, and what the source of these problems is. Generally, every problem we have in our life has a source within us — a thought, a memory, a belief or negative pattern. When the pattern is healed, the problems are gone.
   - OR -
3. **Ask your spirit guide to help you with this spiritual journey. Ask the guide to show you the source of your current problems or the things that you should heal at the current moment of your life.**
4. Now, when you've set the intention, let go of control and observe. Your mind will — either within seconds or after a few minutes — show you images. Memories, interpretations of beliefs, past

events, people, and such. Your task is to observe the images and do an emotional dialog work. Observe the images and analyze your behavior, your reactions, your beliefs. Analyze if they're healthy and good for you or not. If you can see something negative, analyze it as well — see how you have benefitted from a negative experience, and what kind of result it had for your life. Relax and let go of any negative emotions once they're analyzed. Forgive yourself and people you recall if necessary. When the specific image is "worked out," move on — let go and allow the mind to direct you further.
5. If you do work with a spirit guide, and you can communicate with him or her, ask for additional help and advice. Allow the guide to advise you on how to deal with a specific problem.
6. When you're done with the journey, return to the normal world by opening your eyes.

The whole purpose of this spiritual journey is to travel through visions and learn from them. If you stumble upon something difficult — a bad memory, for example — relax and use another technique of healing emotions. Affirmations or core images are a few examples. That's it! You've learned the Psychonaut Method.

Whenever you have problems or just time to grow, sit down and practice this technique of spiritual growth. It will help you resolve your life problems and difficulties. And more than that — through allowing yourself to observe and follow the "visions" and images, you develop your clairvoyance further. This will benefit you in the future, mainly in different forms of psychic readings. The technique itself is quite simple, so practice it whenever you can.

Do Angels Have Wings?

It's time for more theoretical stuff! As you progress with clairvoyance practice, you will be experiencing more and more symbols. Drawings, scenes, types of movement, animals, people, specific colors and such — all these are psychic symbols. And it is important to remember that psychic symbols are subjective, not objective. It means that everyone perceives psychic information in a subjective, personal way. This is why I don't like books that describe the colors of auras in a general way. So before we progress to learning how to view auras and chakras, and how to perform psychic readings, you have to understand a thing or two about symbolism and the importance of your personal dictionary of psychic symbols.

The question "do angels have wings" might sound silly, but when you're clairvoyant, the answer is a bit more complex. How do we perceive angels? Well, subjectively. The very first thing that you need to understand is that we perceive the energetic or spiritual world from our own perspective. It's like the "I say to-*may*-to — you say to-*mah*-to" kind of thing. Whatever you see clairvoyantly will have a meaning to you and only you. You can't ask "I see this and this, what does it mean?" of another psychic because whatever you perceive is being channeled through your own perception filters.

Perception filters are our beliefs, experiences, and knowledge, everything that is stored within our mind. The best way to describe a perception filter is to give an example of colors. In Europe, the color white is a color of purity and peace; it is often worn by brides. In Japan, it's the opposite; white is the color of death and grief. It's all about cultural interpretation. In the same way, it works for the psychic mind. For someone else, the color red might symbolize blood and aggression; for me, red symbolizes passionate strength and even strong love. And that's why you shouldn't trust books that say "this and this color symbolizes this and this" — it does, but only for the book's author. That's why you're going to create your own dictionary of psychic symbols soon.

For now, let's get back to angels. Do they have wings or not? Well, yes they do. But what's more important is how we perceive them, rather than what they really look like. If we're talking about angels already, let's continue this example. To me, Archangel Raphael has short brown hair and wears jeans. When he comes to my room, he often carries leaves and pine needles with him. I can see these on the floor. Archangel Michael is tall with long hair and wears awesome metal armor. My own spirit guide has short black hair and wears something like a black leather jacket. And yet, all of this is subjective — it goes through my own perception filters. Quite often it's the case that different people perceive them in similar ways. It's interesting to look at modern "psychic" paintings of Raphael and see that other people perceive him in almost the same way I do. But this is just the case of spiritual beings.

When an entity is conscious, it has a tendency to project its form to the minds of people, so we, as psychics, perceive these beings in a similar way. They want us to see them in this way and not another. If they want us to see wings, we will see wings. But even if they project their form (which they don't have, really, it's just a projection — after all, they're spiritual beings) our perception can vary. A friend of mine has wings — he's an incarnated nature spirit. Some people perceive these wings as butterfly wings, like in all these Irish stories of good fairies. And I perceive these wings as strong searchlights in the mist directed towards the sky. I can see wings — but my perception is slightly different.

Whenever you perceive something (for example an entity) in a manner different from someone else, don't worry — really. The perception is subjective, and it can vary from person to person. And sometimes a couple of psychics can see the same thing. One time, I was sitting in a room with a friend, and I saw two energetic cats walk into the room. And I asked, "Umm, what can you see here?" She said, "Two cats." I said, "They're very lean, aren't they?" And my friend said, "Indeed." Such small experiences prove to me that clairvoyance is real.

The Clairvoyant Symbols Dictionary

Anyway, spirit beings are one thing. Symbols, that's another thing. Symbols are often very, very subjective. I've mentioned colors already, but it's much wider than that. Through our lives we read many books, see many movies, see many symbols, and so on. All of this creates our experience. And when we stumble upon similar energies, meanings, or causes during our psychic practice, for example, during psychic readings, our mind translates the psychic impressions into images (symbols) familiar to us. That's why it's very important to interpret your clairvoyant vision during psychic readings, aura reading, and chakra reading by yourself.

I mention this because there are many books available that explain the meanings of different things that can be seen within the aura or chakras, books explaining each chakra and their meanings, and books that contain explanations of psychic symbols. Should you read such books? Well, yes — because they give you additional knowledge of symbols, chakras, auras, and things that you can experience during your clairvoyant practice. But in the end, as you study such books, remember that you're solely responsible for the interpretation of the things you see.

That is why during each reading it's mandatory to ask YOURSELF "What does THIS mean to ME?" Your own interpretation matters. Your mind will give you explanations, and you will understand things you see with time and practice. And as you progress with your clairvoyant practice, you will receive more visions, more symbols. So it's a good idea to create your own dictionary of clairvoyant symbols.

Therefore, prepare a notebook. And after each Psychonaut Method journey, after each visit in your clairvoyant laboratory, and after each aura, chakra, or psychic reading, write all new symbols and meanings in the notebook. With time, such a notebook will become a useful resource for your psychic work. Start writing the dictionary right now and include all the symbols and visions that you experience; then write all your feelings, emotions, and your own understanding of the things you have seen.

At first you can work with your own visions/symbols. From time to time, return to previous entries and re-read them. Analyze if some of the visions seem to be more understandable over time, or which interpretation seems to be most accurate. With time, you will learn how to interpret the symbol correctly. Later on, as you start working with other people, ask them to provide you with feedback after some time so you can check your interpretations of clairvoyant images as well. This way, you will improve your own psychic skills.

Seeing Auras

Now that you have learned more about symbols and ways that we perceive spiritual beings, we can learn more about seeing auras. Then, I will teach you how to perform a chakra reading, and finally, we will proceed to the practice of entire psychic readings.

The aura is an energy field that emanates from the body of every living being — animals, plants, and humans, too. Some auras are stronger, while others are weaker; some are bright, while others are dirty and require some psychic cleansing. But they're there, always. There are many ways to perceive an aura — most tutorials teach how to perceive auras through physical clairvoyance, but I will teach you how to perceive an aura through your inner sight. For this practice, you won't be using the clairvoyant laboratory. Instead, you will be using just pure clairvoyance — you will sit, and observe, just like that.

You already know what inner sight is — it's an additional layer of perception generated by your mind that looks similar to dreams and visualization. And once your Third Eye is open, you can use the inner sight quite easily. So now you're going to practice it. What you need is a practice partner. It can be a plant, an animal, or a person. Choose one — because in all cases, the way you use the inner sight is exactly the same. Only the details vary. Plants have a simple aura; animals have more complex auras because they're more conscious. And people have very complex auras since we're sentient spiritual beings. But don't worry about this now.

How to See Auras Through Inner Sight

Anyway, let's get to the tutorial itself.

1. Sit down and relax. You might want to close your eyes if you're a beginner. But the more you practice, the easier it will be to focus with your eyes open. For now, close them and enter the alpha state.
2. Look at your target if your eyes are open, or imagine the target, visualize it, if your eyes are closed — the target can be a plant, an animal, or a person. All you have to do is create a focal point. Looking at someone, or visualizing him or her, is such a focal point, the "hook" that I already have mentioned.
3. With your focal point, the hook, in your mind, visualize the aura — a bright energy field around the person. Simply visualize it, and then, after a few seconds — let go.
4. Once you let go, just observe. Allow your inner sight to show you the true aura. If your Third Eye is open enough, you will notice the change in your inner sight perception. The size of the aura might change, and the colors will be different, and you might start noticing additional elements of the aura.
5. So, just observe, pay attention, but do not struggle — allow yourself to see and not to create.
6. When you're done with observation, relax, stop looking, and cut the energy cord (link) that you created.

That's it — that's how you perceive auras of objects and people and animals through your inner sight. First, you create the focal point, the hook, by looking at something or visualizing the target. Then, you visualize the aura of the target, and then you let go. The inner sight, if it's developed nicely, will pick up, and you will be able to see the aura. If you can't see anything, keep practicing — and remember, do not struggle and do not force yourself to see. Once you're relaxed and once you let go for real, you will see.

If you wish, you can ask "control questions" — such questions are another way of creating a point of focus, a hook, to which your psychic intuition will assign visual information. For example, when you observe the aura, ask yourself with an intention of seeing and receiving the answer: How big is the aura? What color dominates in this particular aura? Is there anything extraordinary within this aura? Are there any specific layers within the aura? You can ask any question you want, and then simply wait for your intuition to give you answers. The more questions you ask, the more answers you receive, and the better your clairvoyance becomes.

Now that you know how to see the aura, you can grab some books that explain different layers of auras and different things that you can see within the aura. For example, you can see darker pieces of the aura where the energy field is damaged, or where some nasty energy attached itself, and it requires cleansing. Or you might see scratches on the aura, or additional layers and such. All of this is so complex that it would require a few more books about the subject. But even if you can't get the books, don't worry — I'm here to teach you something, right? But I won't be teaching you about aura layers or different things that you can see within an aura — I already taught you this. The simplicity of learning is great because the only thing you really need is your own intuition. Whenever you see something upon the aura, or within chakras, as you will learn later on, ask yourself what it means, what this new thing that you see means. Through your intuition, the mind will give you the answer, and you will learn something new. It's that simple!

Once you can see, use your own intuition to learn what the things you see means. It's how every single psychic in the world learns the meanings of auras. Now you can learn about something that lies below the aura — chakras.

The Chakra Reading

The chakras are energy centers within our body. There are seven primary chakras that are relevant to chakra reading. And a chakra reading is a psychic analysis of all seven chakras that helps understand blockages, so a person can quickly learn what areas of life should be fixed first before proceeding with spiritual growth further. As I said, there are seven main chakras. Here they are:

1. The Root Chakra — Maladhara

This is the first chakra, also known as "the base." It is located at the base of the spine. Is has only one opening, pointing downwards. This chakra is related to the spinal column and kidneys, and governs the adrenal glands. It's the rooted, physical part of our being, governing survival and primal instincts. It's how we respond to our own body and the nature around us. In simple words, it says, "Eat, don't allow to be eaten."

2. The Sexual Chakra — Swadisthana

Known also as the navel or the sacral chakra, located just below the navel. This is the first chakra that opens both front and back. It's related to the reproductive system, and the glands affected are the gonads. Yes, this chakra is related to sexuality, and additionally to relationships with others. It's not just about sex, but more about the ability to form intimate bonds, not necessary sexual. You can describe it as "**I want to be** with this person."

3. The Personality Chakra — Manipura

The solar plexus chakra, located below the breastbone and slightly to the left. It opens front and back and controls the stomach, liver, gall bladder, and nervous system. It's about willpower, determination, and personality. It's about your destiny and the way you fit into the world. You can describe it as "this is my partner, this is my home."

4. The Heart Chakra — Anahata

This chakra is located in proximity to the heart, and it's responsible for emotions. It opens front and back, and it's responsible for bringing emotions to your life. It primarily controls your heart, lungs, and blood. The best way to describe this chakra is to phrase it as "I like that female, she means something to me, I feel something towards her." This chakra is also responsible for improving your control over psychic abilities. Pay attention to it.

5. The Expressive Chakra — Vissudha

The chakra of communication controls your entire throat and communication capabilities. "I'm telling you, I want to marry this girl" — with these words, we describe this chakra, as it's all about communicating our will towards the world around us. You can have your will to shape your life, but if you have problems with the fifth chakra, you won't be able to turn your will into action.

6. The Third Eye (Knowledge Chakra)

Anja, the famous "Third Eye." This chakra governs out intuition and steers our psychic abilities. It also controls our brain and everything that we can find within. This chakra is responsible for showing us the world as it really is — and it's also an important energy center when it comes to inner growth, as it allows us not only to see things around us, but also things within us.

7. The Crown Chakra — Sahasraha

This chakra is often associated with white, purple, or gold colors. And all I can tell you about this chakra is that it's purely focused on our spirituality, connecting us to higher values, to the "source," which some call God.

Sahasraha
the crown chakra

Ajna
the third eye chakra

Vissudha
the throat chakra

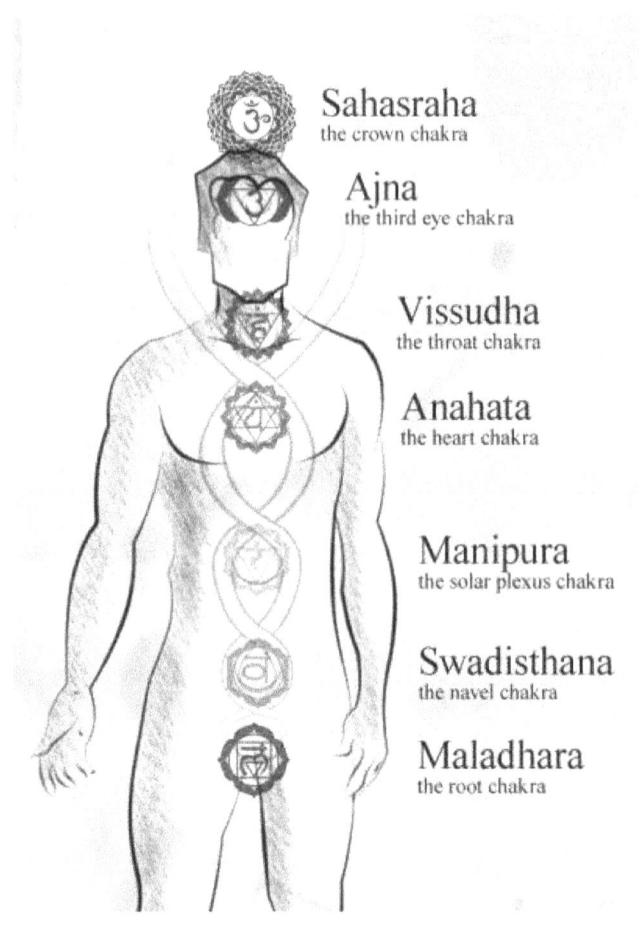

Anahata
the heart chakra

Manipura
the solar plexus chakra

Swadisthana
the navel chakra

Maladhara
the root chakra

The school of chakras originates from Hindu beliefs, and they were transferred to Western ground through Theosophy. If you're a Wiccan, or a pagan, or anyone from a different tradition that doesn't believe in chakras, you don't have to see them — you might, or you might not. I know a couple of people who don't believe in chakras, but they can see them. Often, chakras are considered by these people as metaphors of inner personalities — and they can be used for psychological analysis of a person. Whether you believe in chakras or not, try to see them — if you do see them, use this knowledge to help others, but if you can't see them, that's okay, too — especially if chakras do not fit your point of view.

Anyway, I have decided to teach you aura viewing first, and then go to chakras, for an important reason. With this order, you're going to learn how to switch layers of perception. The entire process of perceiving chakras is exactly the same as the process of perceiving aura. So let's do some copy-paste with additional points. Do not be surprised if you can't see chakras on plants, and there are fewer chakras in the case of animals. Seven chakras exist in humans only.

I recall the first time I was able to see the inside energetics and the chakras. I asked my training partner to sit and relax, and I focused on her. Then, I closed my eyes and I visualized the chakras, and finally, I let go of control. Then, the chakras that I visualized changed! They moved a bit, almost as if they tried to fit the proper area of the body where they should be located. Some of them glowed strongly, while others were weaker. And I could see the primary energy channels that go in proximity to the spine from the root chakra to the tip of the head. It was a truly extraordinary experience!

How to Do a Chakra Reading

Here's the tutorial itself:

1. Sit down and relax. You might want to close your eyes if you're a beginner. But the more you

practice, the easier it will be to focus with your eyes open. For now, close them and enter the alpha state.
2. Look at your target if your eyes are open, or imagine the target, visualize it, if your eyes are closed — the target can be a plant, an animal, or a person. All you have to do is create a focal point. Looking at someone, or visualizing him or her, is such a focal point, the "hook" that I already have mentioned.
3. With your focal point, the hook, in your mind, visualize the aura — a bright energy field around the person. Simply visualize it and then, after few seconds — let go.
4. Once you let go, just observe. Allow your inner sight to show you the true aura. If your Third Eye is open enough, you will notice the change in your inner sight perception. The size of the aura might change, or the colors will be different, and you might start noticing additional elements of the aura.
5. So, just observe, pay attention, but do not struggle — allow yourself to see and not to create.
6. **Here is where chakra reading starts. Once you see the aura, switch the layer of perception. Visualize all the seven chakras and intend to perceive them. Ignore the aura completely and focus on the chakras. Once you're done, let go. Allow the inner sight to show you the chakras of the person. After a few moments, you should see them.**
7. Then, simply observe.
8. When you're done with observation, relax, stop looking, and cut the energy cord (link) that you created.

That's it — once you can see the chakras, everything else is a matter of perception and analysis based on the intuitive work and personal understanding of things that you can see. You can see that some chakras glow strongly while others glow weakly; some might be bigger than others; within some chakras, there might be some additional symbols or things included.

Once again, you can ask the control questions for additional hooks to which your psychic intuition will assign answers: Which chakras are stronger, and which chakras are weaker? What colors can I see within *this* particular chakra? Are there any blockages or additional energetic structures within *this* particular chakra? Which chakras require balancing, and which chakras require cleansing? Ask, and the answer shall be given to you!

I once saw a weird pattern of regular lines within the chakra of a person. I interpreted it, correctly, as a form of psychic shield, allowing some energies in and keeping some energies out. The person confirmed that such a shield had been placed on the chakra for spiritual purposes. Today, as a Reiki practitioner, I can often perceive the Reiki signs embedded within the chakras of other Reiki practitioners, simply because I know what to look for.

The chakras have been nicely described in detail in my other book *Psychic Development Simplified*, and in *The Chakra* Handbook by Bodo Baginski, which I strongly recommend. But again, it's all about your intuition — observe the chakras and everything that you can see within them, and your intuition will tell you what you see. That's it. You've learned how to perceive the chakras.

Now that I've taught you how to see auras and chakras, there's something interesting that I want to mention. In most cases, it's difficult to perceive your own aura and your own chakras. It's funny, almost ironic, that even if we can perceive auras and chakras of others, most of us have troubles perceiving our own chakras and aura. This is normal at first, and maybe with time you can rebuild your mind to such a degree that you won't have too many mental blockages to block you from looking at yourself from an energetic perspective. Anyway, that's why it's a good idea to have friends that are also clairvoyant, so they can look at you if you have something attached to your aura, or when there are problems with your chakras.

Perceiving Inner Energetics

The energy body of a person or animal is made of meridians (energy channels) and chakras (energy centers). All these can be perceived through clairvoyance in a similar way as you perceive chakras and the entire aura. All you have to do is to switch the perception. Intend to see the meridians and inner energetic systems beyond chakras, and within a few moments, you should be able to see them. You will perceive blockages of a different sort, or attachments, and things like this. An ability of perceiving the inner energetics is very useful for every person that is interested in psychic healing or Reiki practice.

Also, you can perceive the energetics of internal organs: heart, lungs, kidneys, and such. To do so, all you have to do is, once again, switch the layer of clairvoyant perception. Visualize all the internal organs and attach the aura to them, visualize their aura. Then simply let go. Within a few moments, you will be able to perceive the energetics of the inner organs. Generally, the organs that lack energy will be darker, and the healthy organs will glow nicely. Of course, the way you recognize if the organ is energized or not, healthy or ill, is subjective. So learn your own symbols of perception.

Again, remember to ask control questions — the more questions you ask, the more answers you will receive, and the more detailed your psychic reading and clairvoyant perception becomes.

Just remember — the ability to perceive organs can be useful for psychic healers and Reiki practitioners, but as long as you're not a doctor, do not give any kind of medical diagnosis.

More Theoretical Tips

As you progress with clairvoyant development in practical aspects — meaning, that when you begin practicing the actual clairvoyance — you will still charge the Third Eye, and it will get cleansed and healed. Because of this, with time more memories, patterns, and negative thoughts might appear in your conscious mind. When they do, use affirmations or core images or any other technique to work these out and heal your emotions. This will improve your clairvoyance, and it will also improve your daily life.

Remember another thing: clairvoyant vision uses energies, our life force, Chi. The more you look around, the more energies you burn; they're like fuel. So don't look all the time, especially when you still are a beginner. Manage your energies wisely and implement some kind of spiritual practice to recharge your psychic batteries. For example, learn Tai Chi Chuan or Qigong, or become a Reiki practitioner. Other methods of charging your psychic batteries include eating healthy food with a lot of fresh vegetables, getting good and peaceful sleep, rest, and meditation. When you're tired, don't look around — simply don't let yourself burn out completely.

There is one more thing you need to keep in mind — learning to see won't allow you to see only spirits, ghosts, and some wicked energies. You will see both bad and good stuff. But more than that, you will see the problems people have. And finally, you will see the problems you have. Seeing is an element of spiritual growth, and spiritual growth is something that requires us to face our true self. In order to do so, we must face the illusion we've created around ourselves. And this may be painful for many. In simple words, you won't see only ghosts, but you will see your own lies, attachments, problems, and karma issues, the dirty stuff you wanted to forget about. But it's there, and seeing it allows you to heal yourself, and work things out. Keep this in mind. Seeing is "cool," but using this ability for your own inner growth is even better.

Doing Psychic Readings

Now it's time to get back to the clairvoyant laboratory and teach yourself how to perform a clairvoyant psychic reading. Actually, I already had explained what the psychic reading looks like when I taught you about the clairvoyant laboratory. It's not difficult, but I will explain it one more time. A psychic reading is one of the most popular uses of psychic perception in the world. In short words, it's a process in which information is collected via psychic means, and then it's provided to another person.

Remember the safety rules. Ground and center yourself, cleanse yourself after each reading, especially between readings, and remember to light a candle during the reading.

How to Perform a Psychic Reading

Now, let's get to the tutorial itself. Let's say you have a client who wishes to receive a reading. The first question is, "Does this person ask a specific question or just want to know what's wrong with his or her life?" In the first case, you're going to look for the answer to the specific question, and in the second case, you're going to look for any tips or messages that might be useful for the person who wants your psychic reading. So, let's begin.

1. **Ground and Center** — when you perform a psychic reading, you will receive energies from the person. So ground yourself, visualize the energetic roots coming from your feet and going into the ground, and intend them to release all unnecessary or negative energies back to the ground automatically. Then, center yourself. Focus on the lower Tan T'ien for a while, then focus on the Third Eye. This time, it's a bit different because you need more energies within your Third Eye to work with.
2. **Connect with the person** — you need to create a link. To do so, intend to connect with the person, just like that. It will work because energy follows thoughts. If you wish, you can visualize a peaceful cord of energy coming from your body and touching the body of the other person in front of you. Think, "I wish to connect with the person in front of me," and you will get the connection, as well.
3. **Enter the clairvoyant laboratory** — now, go to your clairvoyant laboratory. Close your eyes, relax, enter the alpha state, and see your lab. With time

and practice, and with more experience, you won't have to close your eyes. You will just relax and be able to remain with eyes open, and yet, you'll be able to see your lab and perform your psychic work. It takes some practice and time but be patient.

4. **Start asking questions** — now, ask the question. If the customer has a specific question, ask it. If he's a general client, then just allow your intuition to show you the things that he wishes to know.

5. **Receive** — and when you keep the goal in your mind, when you know what you wish to know about the person or the person's problems, just observe and start receiving. Trust your intuition. Just as you were practicing the Psychonaut Method, allow yourself to be guided by your intuition and observe the images and visions that come to you. Then, interpret them. Perform the interpretation as in any other case — with aura or chakra, simply trust your intuitive thoughts and understanding of the things that you see.

6. **Relay the answer** — relay the answer or any information to the client. It might pull you out from your relaxation, but don't worry. Enter the alpha state again if you need to. With time, it will become a lot easier to perform the reading and talk to the person at the same time. At first, you might need to enter the lab, then get back to the real world, and relay the answer to the client. Don't worry about it, especially if you still are a beginner.

7. **Cut the link** — if the client doesn't have any more questions, end the reading and cut the link with the person.

8. **Ground and Center again** — ground yourself again, and then center and focus on the lower Tan T'ien and direct all energies that aren't needed elsewhere to this area of your energy body. Finally, when the reading is done, cleanse yourself because each time you connect with someone, you collect this person's energies of a different sort, so regular cleansing is important.

You should cut the link at the end of the entire psychic reading session. You don't have to cut it after each and every visit in your clairvoyant laboratory, just after you're done with the person you've read.

Beware! During a reading, you might accidentally receive a communication from spirits — ghosts. If you're not a skilled psychic and you know little about psychic self-defense, remember to shield yourself and ask your spirit guide for protection, even if you do not believe in spirit guides. If you're not skillful enough, refuse any form of spirit communication — just shout in your mind "no!" and if the spirit is aggressive, break the connection with the client and end the reading. Spirit communication is a more advanced subject, and I don't feel experienced enough to discuss it.

If you wish, you can perform psychic readings, or aura and chakra readings, at a distance. It's useful to know that, in the world of energies, there's no such thing as distance. In order to perform the reading at a distance (and you can read objects and places at a distance, too), you need a target — something that will mentally connect you with the person or place you wish to read. For example, a photo — it can be physical or digital. Or you might want to use the person's voice over the phone or Skype. Or you can use an e-mail address and person's name. These are so-called "coordinates" — and trust me, they will work. When I offer psychic services at a distance, I usually require the e-mail address and customer's PayPal data to get the connection. It may sound difficult, but it's quite simple.

You look at the photo or e-mail address, and you think to yourself, "I wish to connect psychically with that person," and you're done — you're connected. Remember, you need to cut the link at the end of the reading session even if you read at a distance. Distance matters not on the spiritual plane.

And that's how you perform the psychic reading. As a beginner, it's a great idea to practice psychic readings and other forms of readings (aura, chakra) with friends or family members. Use them as guinea pigs (of course, ask them if they agree, first), and ask them for their feedback. Their feedback for your psychic findings will help you learn to work with intuition, interpretations, and with the clairvoyance itself.

Now, whenever you do a psychic reading, or aura reading, or even chakra reading, do not focus on visual perception only. At the beginning of this book, I mentioned that, in most cases, clairvoyance acts as a primary psychic sense that often is supported by additional senses. So, keep an open mind. During the clairvoyant reading, you might experience clairaudience, feelings, intuitive messages, and you might simply "know things." That's okay. Use all this additional psychic perception to improve yourself as a psychic.

Beware, Again!

When you practice clairvoyance, practice it with a willing partner only, please. It's because whenever you look at a person you create an energy cord, a link that connects you with that person. And some people like their privacy; they don't like if someone is observing them. It's like looking at a person in the shower — not very ethical, is it? Most people won't realize that you're looking at them clairvoyantly, but you never know who you might stumble upon.

If the person is a psychic or an occultist, he might consider your observation as a form of psychic attack, and he might defend himself through attacking you. So, please, be careful and practice only with people that are willing to do so.

Practicing Clairvoyance Through Observation

Now that you know a lot of practical skills like aura viewing or chakra and psychic reading, I can provide you with some additional exercises and examples that will help you with the development of your own clairvoyant abilities. There's a lot of things that you can observe through clairvoyance. You can use rooms, objects, crystals, and your garden outside to practice clairvoyance; you can develop this ability even if you don't have access to a training partner.

In all the following situations, you need to use the technique that you have learned in the aura viewing and chakra reading tutorial. You focus on a hook — an object — or you visualize it, if you prefer to perceive things with your eyes closed. Then, you visualize the aura and the energetics. And finally, you let go. Within a few moments, you can perceive the energies of the target.

Things You Can Practice With

First, you can observe every single object you can think of. The mighty collection of kitchen knives; the books on the shelf; the furniture, too. Every single object around you can be observed via clairvoyance because every single object contains some kind of energy. How is it different from auras? Well, auras are energy fields generated by living beings. Objects glow psychically because they collect energies from their environment. So you can see if an object is energized with positive energies, or if it contains dark, unpleasant energies.

You can perceive and practice with talismans, amulets, and different types of sacred symbols. All these give some kind of "visible" energy. Visible through clairvoyance, of course. With time, you will be able to distinguish whether the kind of energy you see is positive, spiritual, or whether the energy that you see is unpleasant, negative, and requires cleansing.

If you wish, you can perceive entire rooms and buildings. They glow as well — at least those that are cleansed and filled with spiritual energies, for example, temples or sacred spaces in which a person meditates or performs some kind of spiritual work. You can use this skill to analyze which room in the building requires some psychic cleansing.

If you have access to a sacred place, for example, a sacred mountain or sacred forest, take a look at it, as well. A word of warning here — if a place gives you the creeps and is said to be haunted, then, please, don't look around, you'll be safer this way. But if you know that a place is a sacred place, a power place, then take a look — you might be surprised to realize how strong it glows.

You can practice clairvoyance by observing crystals. There are different types of crystals. Bring some types of crystals together and look at them, try to notice the subtle differences in their energetics. Then leave a crystal for a few weeks in the room in which you, for example, work, and look at it after these few weeks. Notice if the energetic changed; maybe the crystal is darker, maybe it collected some negative energies? Then cleanse the crystal; place it in salt water for 24 hours or bury it in the garden for 24 hours. Then take a look again. Does it look different? Maybe it's cleansed, cleaner? It should be!

Our world is a beautiful place . Go outside and observe the energetics of the garden — the grass, all the flowers, the birds that fly around. When I first saw this, it was like sitting in the cinema and watching the *Avatar* movie by James Cameron! So many colors, and it was so real, even if I could see it only through my inner sight. Observe the trees — trees are powerful energy sources. They collect the energy of heaven, the spiritual energy, and they channel it into Mother Earth. And you can see the process, along with the powerful aura of the trees. The trees that are dead won't have a powerful aura, and they will only collect energies instead of generating the auric field as living beings do.

Observe animals, as well . Go to the zoo and look at animals there. Observe the animals that live in your home, if there are any. Cats or dogs, whatever! Don't be surprised if you can perceive a powerful Third Eye chakra in the case of cats. Cats are very, very psychic!

Do Some Exercises

Look at the room you're in right now. What kind of energies can you see? Can you perceive entities, for example, your spirit guide? Are there any negative energies in the room? What does your spirit guide look like? Try to describe him or her. Look at the nearest objects. What kind of energies are they charged with? What colors can you see around you? Just relax, enter an alpha state, focus on your Third Eye, and then look around through your inner sight, and you will be able to perceive the world through clairvoyance.

One more tip that I have for you is to find someone who can "see" as well. Such a person can confirm your clairvoyant findings, and with such a person's help, you can improve the confidence in your own abilities.

Practicing Clairvoyance On-Line

The Internet is a powerful tool of psychic development! There's Facebook, Wikipedia, Flickr, and hundreds of websites that provide you with photos of people, events, places, and objects. You have learned how to perceive the energetics, how to work with the clairvoyant laboratory, and how to perform psychic reading at a distance. You can use this knowledge to practice your clairvoyance further with the use of the Internet!

How to do so? Well, go to Wikipedia, Flickr, Facebook, and any other website that provides you with photos. Choose one photo that you wish. With the photo in mind and in front of you on the screen, close your eyes and relax. Ask yourself, and ask the higher guidance if it's safe for you to connect with the people, places, and events in the photo. If you receive the intuitive answer "yes," which might be just a gut feeling, continue on. If you receive an answer "no," which also might be just a gut feeling, find a different photo.

Then, through your intention, connect with whatever is in the photo. Use your clairvoyant laboratory to analyze the photo. Look at the aura of the place and people, and try to receive as much psychic information about the photo as possible through your laboratory. If you use Wikipedia, it's highly possible that the article to which the photo was attached will provide you with feedback and you will know if you're right or not. In all other cases, if feedback isn't possible, just keep practicing, as in this way, you will develop your clairvoyance further.

You can merge the clairvoyant laboratory and other techniques together. Once in your laboratory, hook a person or an object, visualize it along with its aura, and let go — your inner sight will pick up, and you will be able to observe auras and chakras within the clairvoyant laboratory. And since there are millions of photos out there, then you have a lot to practice with.

Now I've mentioned earlier that you should ask the person you wish to look at for permission. And here I'm telling you to connect with people from photos — is it okay? Indeed, because you've asked for permission — not from the people, but the higher guidance. If it tells you it's okay, then you'll be safe.

A few words of advice, though, regarding this way of learning to see. I've met with the following situation. There are forums (on-line discussion boards) where people post photos of different people and places and ask others to tell what they "feel" or "see." Yes, it's a way to practice clairvoyance and other psychic perception abilities, but let's be honest — it's not the wisest thing to do. Remember, whenever you connect with a person or a place, you create a link through which different beings and energies can follow you back. And unless you're quite good at psychic self-defense, you might get yourself into trouble. If the place or person that you see on a photo feels "bad," don't proceed with any psychic reading or clairvoyant experiment. You'll be safer this way.

One time I was looking at a photo of a haunted cemetery. Experienced paranormal investigators warned everyone about this place. Immediately as I checked it out psychically, I got this evil feeling. It was really evil. I broke the contact with the place right away because whatever gives me such terrible sensations can't be good.

The Clairvoyance Support Circle

Do you want to know how my psychic teacher taught me to see? Now that's an interesting story. I paid her a visit, and we were enjoying a cup of coffee when, suddenly, she said, "Okay, describe my spirit guide." And I said, "What?!" I was completely shocked. "You already can see, now describe my spirit guide," said she. So I did — I just looked around, focused, and engaged my inner sight. And I described the spirit guide. I was correct, and this small experienced proved to me that I can see for real. Other small experiences proved this to me, as well, where there were a couple of people in the room, and we could see the exact same thing together.

That is why I believe that you should create a clairvoyance support circle. Simply gather three or four people who are interested in learning to see and to use clairvoyance and start the practice. Below are some exercises that will help you with a group practice.

Describe the Aura

Each one of you has an aura. The best way to practice is to choose a person whose aura you're going to observe. Then, use your favorite clairvoyance technique and gather the reading and information silently in your mind. Then, when you're ready, you can describe the person's aura and compare your findings. If you wish, you can write down your findings on paper so you won't be "inspired" by each other. Remember to cut the links after you're done.

Describe the Spirit Guide

Another nice exercise is to describe the spirit guide of each member of the support circle. Choose a person whose spirit guide you're going to observe. Just think of the spirit guide and describe him or her. Then again, compare your findings. Now this exercise can be practiced on your own.

Work with Printed Images

You can practice a different form of clairvoyance called Remote Viewing. Let one person prepare a set of a dozen photos — they might be printed, and their source can be the Internet. Place each photo in a separate envelope and let one person be a monitor — someone that will take care of opening and showing the photos.

Let the monitor pick up one photo in the closed envelope. Then, each one of you should connect with the photo and describe it through clairvoyance. When you're done, compare your findings, then let the monitor open the envelope and show the photo.

Charging and Checking Cards

If there is a skilled energy worker among you, he can pick up a deck of cards. Create a few sets of cards, five cards each. Let the energy worker charge one card from each set with psychic energies and then place all the cards from the small deck on the table. Now observe the cards, and choose which card has been charged with energies — it should be the card that glows the most. Then, when each one of you has made the choice, let the energy worker point to the card that has been charged. Of course, the person that charges the card should look at it first to be sure which card has been charged.

Finally, whenever you can sense something, or one person can see something others haven't noticed yet, ask others "what do you see?" Don't describe first, allow everyone to take their "reading" and then compare your findings.

Automatic Clairvoyance and Learning Control

With time, you might notice that clairvoyance pops up on its own — you're doing normal things, and then, suddenly, you can perceive a spirit without any previous meditation or preparation. This is quite normal. At first, it might take some time to relax and be able to perceive things through clairvoyance, but with time, it will get easier and easier. Within a few months, you might start to see right away — almost automatically, even if you do not intend to see. Relax, as this is a normal process of clairvoyant development.

Your clairvoyance might turn on at any time. At first, you might be excited, but it's a good idea to learn a bit of control. So how should you control your clairvoyant abilities? First, when you do not wish to see, remember to ground yourself and center on your lower Tan T'ien — this will bring energies back to this area of your energy body, and your Third Eye won't have enough energy.

You can also intend to stop seeing — simply think "I'm turning my clairvoyance off, I can't see right now." You can also visualize your Third Eye closing. Imagine your Third

Eye as a normal eye that closes with an intention of turning clairvoyance off. You can also set up a psychic shield — just as you learned how to create a defensive shield earlier in this book, create a similar shield, but this time intend it to block all psychic energies that lead to clairvoyant perception.

You can also change the point of focus. When I do not wish to see, I'm thinking about blue ducks on white grass under a red sky. Just visualize something extraordinary, something that will make your brain busy figuring things out — whenever you wish to stop perceiving through clairvoyance, focus on something else, think and visualize something else, something completely unrelated to your clairvoyant perception.

These simple things will help you learn clairvoyance. As with any new skill, they might not be very effective at first, but with time and practice, they will become a proper way of controlling your automatic clairvoyance.

Frequently Asked Questions

While writing this book, I've been asked a few questions from many different people. Interestingly, these questions were very similar; thus, I can see that most people have very similar problems when it comes to learning clairvoyance. This chapter is meant to answer these frequently asked questions.

How Do I Know What I See Is Real?

A difficult question it is — to be honest, I do have similar problems from time to time, even with all my experience. First, you must relax — almost everyone has these problems for the first few years of psychic practice.

There are two suggestions I have for people with such a problem. The first suggestion is the reality check.

Step one: when you receive a clairvoyant messages or images, do the reality check — look at the messages and whole communication from a logical point of view. Is there a logical explanation of the message? For example, you might have seen a symbol from your vision earlier in your life, and now your mind is playing a trick by showing you the image from the past. Or you might have heard a discussion between two people, even unconsciously, and now your mind is creating a visualized image of such a conversation, just because it's what it does. Analyze the messages and visions logically, please. Are there any reasons for which you see something, or perceive something?

Look at your emotional approach to exercise or clairvoyant experience — what results were you expecting? If you have approached the experience with strong emotions, they might influence and change your perception, or even "create" things that aren't there. Remember to meditate and to practice with peace of mind.

Do you have some emotional struggles or thoughts bothering your mind that might have influenced your perception in any way? Analyze the experience and see if your perception might be related to the thoughts bothering your mind at the time. Analyze your emotions, as well. If you believe that you *want* a specific experience to occur — if you want something badly, it might happen. Again, keep an open mind and don't expect anything in particular. If there is no logical explanation for things you see or feel, head for another step.

Step two: what does your heart tell you? Your mind is one thing, but if deep inside you, "in your heart," you feel that the message or vision is genuine and that you're really receiving messages or clairvoyant visions, then trust your inner feelings. Then, go to step three.

Step three: practice! The more you perform a reality check and pay attention to inner feelings for confirmation, the more experienced in distinguishing between your mind and real psychic perception you'll be. It's the process of learning — you look for logical explanations, and you find them; then you notice that nothing happens, the messages turned out to be useless, and everything is fine. That's a lesson; you've learned something. Another time, you find no logical explanation for your perception, and you trust your inner feeling. In the end, the messages turn out to be useful and beneficial, and real. That's a lesson, too. The more lessons you learn, the more experienced you will be in noticing the subtle difference between imagination and clairvoyance.

It's a good idea to keep a diary, a journal of your clairvoyant perception. And from time to time, return to your earlier entries and analyze if they came true or not, or if they have a meaning from the perspective of time. These are lessons, too.

Also, remember that, with enough practice, you will notice that there is a subtle difference between imagination or visualization, and real clairvoyance. And with time and experience, you will be able to distinguish one from another. This subtle difference cannot be explained with words — it's subtle, after all. But after a few months, definitely years, you will notice that you can easily distinguish if what you see is real or just imagined.

Why Can't I See Anything?

What I have learned in all these years of my psychic work is that everyone can see by use of clairvoyance. But not everyone is aware of this simple fact. First, do not struggle with the vision. Do not try to perceive the world through physical clairvoyance — this is a rare and advanced psychic ability. First, remember to use the inner sight — that fascinating, almost abstract inner layer of perception that I taught you in this book. Hook to a target, use your visualization to pre-visualize the aura or energetics of the target, and then let go. Your inner sight will kick in, and you will see clairvoyantly.

All you have to do is "intend to see," and the first image that pops up in your inner sight represents the energetic world around you. The longer you focus, the more difficult it is to perceive the energies as they are. Why so? Because the more you focus, the more filters you add to the world you see. You add your own interpretations, beliefs, thoughts, desires, and so on. One of the most important things to learn in regard to psychic perception is to judge not. You must observe, not analyze. The more you analyze, the more blurred the reality of energies become. Of course, you will have to analyze the images, but the analysis goes next — first, you perceive without struggle and analysis. Then, when you have acknowledged the image, the vision, start the analysis, the interpretation that goes through your heart and intuition, and not through your logical mind — your brain. With time, you will learn to do so.

But also, remember that your Third Eye must be open and energized. So remember not to jump into the practice of clairvoyance right away. Spend a few months practicing general psychic development, and then practice a few more months with Third-Eye opening and healing. Then, start the practice of clairvoyance. Finally, remember to rebuild your beliefs about clairvoyance.

I Don't Believe That I Can Do Clairvoyance...

That's a serious problem. If you do not believe you can do clairvoyance, you won't be able to do this. First, you must believe. For this purpose, I have taught you how to use the affirmations. They can be a serious pain in the back, as they can take a year or two to work your blockages and beliefs out, but this practice is worth it. Trust me — if your subconscious mind won't believe that you can do clairvoyance, then no practice or psychic development will help you out. So, please, practice affirmations.

How to Distinguish One Entity from Another

That's a tricky one. Generally, remember what I have said in this book — entities project their form to our minds on their own. For example, entities that belong to the group of fire elementals, salamanders, look nearly the same in all cases. They can be easily distinguished from, let's say, angels. Angels, on the other hand, have different forms — but in most cases for people in the Western world, they look human. They do have wings — sometimes they show them, sometimes they keep the wings hidden. The Bodhisattva Avalokiteśvara looks like a bright, glowing cloud of white and orange light, with a beautiful, woman-like face. But this is how I see this particular Bodhisattva. Yet these are light beings. More evil entities can project positive-looking forms while they're negative in nature. For example, an incubus/succubus, which doesn't have a gender, might project an image of a sexy male or female in order to have energetic sex with a physical person.

Basically, there are two steps in learning how to distinguish one entity from another. The first step is the process of gathering knowledge, and the second step is learning to use your heart and intuition.

So first, learn a lot about different spiritual entities, both the positive and negative ones. Most people perceive them in a similar fashion, so you can learn what to look for in these entities in order to distinguish one from another. Secondly, learn to use your heart and intuition — when you perceive an entity, do not rely only on your clairvoyance, but feel the entity — energetic feelings and intuitive thoughts can rarely be faked, and if you can listen closely with your mind at peace, you can distinguish if the entity is positive or negative. But this takes time to learn, as well.

Therefore, it's a great idea to have someone more experienced to call for help when needed, and consult your own perception with such an experienced person. And, finally, remember to start small. Learn how to trust your intuition through the simple Psychonaut Method and clairvoyant laboratory, then practice, practice, practice with simple things before you decide to start observing entities of a different sort.

How Do I Trust the Information I Receive?

Once again, remember the reality check. Look for logical explanations first. If there aren't any, feel what your heart and intuition tell you. Then, keep practicing and gain more experience. With time, you will learn how to connect these three things together, and you will be able to distinguish the real stuff from the imagined stuff. Trust cannot be created — it has to be earned. And you earn the trust for your own abilities when they come true or when they're confirmed by other psychics. So keep practicing and gain experience.

What if I'm Beginning to See Physically?

Bad news — I don't know how to shut down the physical clairvoyance, so if you don't like it, I can't help you. Good news — it's much easier to work with clairvoyance if you can see entities physically. First of all, don't panic and remember the reality check. Also, go see a doctor. No, really! Most people I know do not see physically, and they use inner sight for clairvoyance. Physical seeing, especially at first, when you can't see entities and energies but flashes or small things like lights, shadows, and such, might suggest problems with your eyes or brain. So check your overall health, first.

If doctors can't find anything wrong with you, then you can consider that you're beginning to see physically. In such a case, simply practice the techniques that I've described in this book, but instead of using your inner sight, use the physical sight. Physical clairvoyance won't harm you, and with a bit of training, you will learn to control when you wish to see things.

Summary

You have learned a lot of theory and many practical techniques for working with clairvoyance. At first, all of this might seem to be chaotic, but don't worry. Just practice everything step by step. Start with theory, practice affirmations and Third-Eye opening, and remember about healing negative mind patterns. Then, head over the practice of aura view, chakra reading, and psychic reading. Practice for a few months, preferably with close friends or family members who can provide you with feedback. And after a few months of such practice, all of this that I've explained and taught in this book will be much easier to understand.

As with everything else, clairvoyance is a skill that seems difficult at first, but with time, you'll finally understand what inner sight is and how to trigger it easily; you will laugh at yourself, thinking, "Damn, now this is EASY!"

Keep yourself safe and enjoy!

Appendix A — Core Images Work

This is a passage taken directly from *Psychic Development Simplified*. It's a detailed tutorial for core images work.

Now we can move to a more effective method of dealing with your blockages. Cleansing your subconscious, thus also removing energy body blockages, can be performed through many different techniques, like affirmations, which you already know. Personally, I use a technique that I call "emotional healing work." This technique is based on the teachings of Robert Bruce, with some modifications made by myself. The essence of the technique is called "core images," and the overall core images work has been mixed by me with Silva's method and auto-programming meditation. This technique can help you deal with negative past memories and experiences very fast and easily. As you should already know, dealing with your past is an important step in psychic development and personal growth.

The Problem Lies in Blockages

Every bad memory or experience or negative pattern creates blockages on energy channels (meridians) or chakras, thus the energy cannot flow freely, and thus, your chakras cannot return to a proper balance.

This always results in problems with psychic abilities — either you cannot develop your psychic sensitivity, or you can't hear your intuition, or no psychic abilities work for you. Some people don't have this problem, as their blockages are minor. But some people get huge blockages that block their psychic development path for good. But not only that. Subconscious blockages can also block your efforts to run a successful business or have a successful relationship, or achieve your personal goals or dreams.

This is why it's important to deal with your subconscious blockages — not only to improve your overall psychic abilities, but also to improve your life and allow you to make a few steps on the path of personal growth. You already know a great technique to deal with your problems — affirmations. But affirmations can be a slow tool. Core images, on the other hand, are very, very fast because they hit the source of your problems directly.

I need to post a disclaimer here. Not everyone will benefit from emotional healing work. Everyone is different, and some people might have trouble with breathing, relaxation, visualization, and so on. Some people might have other blockage that make it impossible to use core images work. How so? For example, you might have been taught that such "mind programming" is just a trick, and it doesn't really work. In such a case, emotional healing won't work because of your belief. Therefore, you will have to write down affirmations to remove that blockage in order to start working with core images later.

Still, try it anyway — because there's no way of knowing if this technique works for you if you don't try it.

Healing Your Emotions

What do you need to start working with core images? Well, at least these things: some free time, peace and quiet, and a dark room or something to cover your eyes because darkness improves your relaxation. And, of course, you need to relax on a comfortable chair or bad. Finally, you need core images to work.

Preparing the List of Core Images

The term "core images" refers to all negative patterns (beliefs, opinions), memories, and experiences you have. These images not only create blockages, but often they can act as attachment points for astral entities and psychic vampires, and it's a good idea to remove them in order to get rid of vampiric attachments and astral beings that feed on you. In order to work with core images, you need to be aware of them, and you need to create a list of them.

Therefore, prepare a notebook in which you're going to write down your images. This can be the same notebook that you're using as your psychic journal, or it can be a completely different notebook. When your notebook is ready, you need to start identifying your core images.

- When you write down affirmations, on the right page of your notebook also write down your emotional responses. Sometimes, you might recall a bad memory or belief like "no, no, life is difficult." Your bad memory is the core image to work with, and your belief is a message that someone taught you, that life is difficult, and you have to recall the memory of that "lesson."
- When you do something, and suddenly you recall some memory that brings an emotional charge with it that is a negative charge, like sadness, aggression, depression, or fear, then this memory is a core image.
- Any negative memory you have creates core images to work with. If someone punched you when you were a child, then it's a core image. When you lost your favorite toy as a child, it's a core image. When your boyfriend broke up with

you and he brought emotional pain, it's a core image. This creates negative belief patterns: a beating might have created a belief that people are only waiting to punch you; losing your toy might result in a fear of losing in the future; heartbreak as a teenager will create relationship problems in the future.
- Any negative pattern you have can be traced back to a negative memory or experience. Just observing your behavior is a good way to identify your core images. Ask yourself why you behave this way. For example, imagine that you've met a nice lady; she's kind, good-looking, and intelligent, but you're afraid to talk to her. Ask yourself, "Why am I afraid to talk with her?" During a core images work session, try to recall your very first memory when you had a problem talking to a girl (you will learn how to recall memories in just a few moments) — et voila, you got your core image.
- Observe your dreams — keeping a dream journal is always a good thing to do, and dreams can carry information about core images for you. Observe your dreams and pay attention to any experiences from the past that might occur to you in a dream state. Write them down, even if they're not true memories but typical dreams — work with dreams then, as they might also help you remove some blockages and negative patterns.
- Sometimes, different events in your life might trigger negative memories — buying a new car, meeting a new person, getting a new job, etc. Pay attention to all memories and emotions that come to you each day.

Continue to work on your core images list — it might contain a few points, or a few hundred points; it doesn't really matter. A word of advice — do not worry if you have hundreds of things to work with. Work with them point by point and be patient. Worrying will only generate new core images to work with in the future. Think about big lists in a positive manner. Think — you now know what you need to deal with. Think that with this big list you have, you will soon deal with all your problems and your life will change within a few months.

Emotional Healing Work Session

Now that you have your list of core images, it's time to have your first work session. So find some time to relax in a quiet, dark place, or use something to cover your eyes. Darkness will help you relax. Sit down or lie in a comfortable position. Remember the first few points from your list — one, two, maybe even five. Don't push yourself, five images per session are enough. Personally, I'm working with a maximum of three core images per session.

Now, follow the procedure carefully. Be sure no one will disturb your peace for the next half an hour.

1. You have to close your eyes and relax all your muscles. Now you have to start breathing — take deep breaths. Breathe in and breathe out fast, one second to breathe in, and one second to breathe out. Take from three to ten such breaths, no more. And then, again — relax.
2. Say, "I'm going back with my memory to..." and define the moment of time, the moment when your experience was recorded and is now a memory.

Then observe that entire experience once more. Negative emotions might appear, just observe them. They're no longer in control, so don't be afraid, don't worry. You might want to cry — that's okay, cry. It's an emotional response meant to decrease emotional pain.

3. Observe the event you've just recalled. Relax, don't worry, don't be afraid; just observe it. Say, "I'm observing, and I'm feeling good. I'm relaxed, I'm calm, I'm secure" — and feel good, feel relaxed, feel calm, feel secure. You're in control. Know that what you're observing is the past, and that past cannot hurt you anymore from your current point of view. You're safe.
4. Say, "When I count down from three to zero, my fear/sadness/anger/depression will go away, and I will feel good, relaxed, calm, and secure." Then slowly count down from three to zero, and let go of all your negative emotions. Feel good, relaxed, calm, and secure.
5. Often, some memories might carry an additional belief — that you're responsible for something, or that someone is responsible for something. For example, when you have made a huge mistake, you might think it's all your fault. Or that when someone broke your heart, it's that person's fault. In such a case, forgive yourself or that person. Just say, "I'm forgiving myself …" or "I'm forgiving NAME …," and when forgiving, do this with your heart — really forgive yourself or that specific person. It will be a relief for both of you.
6. Now visualize a beautiful scene — visualize a place you enjoy. For example, I'm visualizing wonderful

plains with high grass, calm and warm wind, at the time of sunset. You need to visualize a scene you enjoy; it might be a romantic sunset, or a peaceful Buddhist temple, or whatever. The point is that this visualized place must feel safe to you. You must feel at peace when looking at this place; you must feel calm, relaxed, and secure. Use your vivid imagination!

7. Now visualize the scene, the event, or experience in question; visualize it as a paper postcard. This postcard is hovering within your peaceful scene that you visualized in the previous step. Then visualize that postcard moving away, and away, and away, until it disappears beyond the horizon.

8. Now visualize the postcard back again; it's hovering in front of you, within your peaceful scene. Visualize that you're holding a blessed sword in your right hand, and a holy flaming torch in your left hand. Use the sword to cut the postcard to pieces. And then use the torch to burn these pieces. Visualize the pieces burning entirely, leaving no trail, and see that beautiful, peaceful scene you've created earlier. Focus on its beauty, and on all the positive emotions the scene brings you. Enjoy it as long as you want.

9. Say, "Thank you that I'm now free." And that's all — you can now open your eyes and end your session, or move to another core image and repeat steps two through seven.

It might look complex, but after a few sessions, you will learn. Each session might take as little as five minutes, or even 30 minutes. Personally, I have never needed a longer session, and I don't advise you to push yourself to the limits. After 30 minutes, end your session. If there are still emotions attached to your core images, just mark that on your list. You will return to this core image next time. Don't push yourself!

How to Recall Memories

In addition, if you've identified a negative pattern but not the core image itself, you might want to use a simple method for recalling a bad memory.

1. You have to close your eyes and relax all your muscles. Now you have to start breathing — take deep breaths. Breathe in and breathe out fast, one second to breathe in, and one second to breathe out. Take from three to ten such breaths, no more. And then, again — relax.
2. Say, "When I count down from three to zero, I will return with my memory to the first time when …" and name the pattern you're working with, for example, "when I was afraid to speak with a girl." Your mind should respond with a memory — it might not be the memory you were seeking, but still, it's a core image of some sort, somehow related to the pattern you're working with. Use it!
3. In the case when you don't receivee any memory, don't worry. After working with some images, you will deal with many blockages, and new images will appear to you. It takes time to fix your subconscious, but it's worth it!

Additional Tips for Working with Core Images

Below are some additional tips for working with core images.

- As I said, sometimes you might end your session and you won't feel relief. On the contrary, you might feel that the core image is not yet cleansed. In that case, don't worry. Some powerful emotions require more time to deal with than weaker emotions. Just return to the specific image during the next session. Use as many sessions to deal with specific images as you need. Remember — you're not a contest, don't rush, be patient, and take your time.
- Core images can be old or very fresh. Work with both types. If you had an argument yesterday, then it's a core image, and it needs to be cleansed as soon as possible. Treat it as any other core image.

Regarding fresh images, I have a story for you from my personal practice:

Recently, I had a minor blockage on my subconscious. I was led by fear, sadness, and anger because my boss didn't pay me this month. These emotions were primary emotions I had, and for some reason it influenced all my additional income. So I decided to use core images and cleanse these fresh emotions that appeared.

I cleansed the negative emotions and freed myself from them, then took a nap. After waking up and checking my email, I was surprised to learn that I had just made a record of daily passive income by selling so many copies of my books.

Some might say it's coincidence, but I've been psychic long enough to understand that coincidences are psychic phenomena as well, and they're not accidental, they're intentional.

Finally, you might ask, "I'm done with the core image — should I feel anything?" Well, you might feel relief. Or you might even sense more energies flowing through specific parts of your body if you're psychic sensitive enough. Or you might notice changes in your daily life. The only thing you should really feel is nothing.

I'll explain. "Nothing" refers to your emotions when consciously recalling a specific core image. That's why you should not destroy your images list. Read it from time to time and recall the events and memories. If you can feel negative emotions, then it means the core image hasn't been cleansed yet, and you still need to work with it. But if you're recalling the event or memory, and you can't feel negative emotions at all, then it means you've successfully dealt with the image and you should be proud.

Everything else, like physical sensations or life changes, are just the result of your work. But there's an important thing I need to say. Sometimes, removing blockages might result in a serious physical response — you might catch the flu, or you might notice a pimple on your face (and it doesn't matter that you're 60 years old), or you might get muscle spasm. Don't worry, this is a good sign; it means that your energy body is working to heal itself. You should see my face today after I dealt with some nasty attachments.

Working with Positive Images

There's one more thing I need to mention — positive core images. These are the images usually related to astral entities and psychic vampires. They're like open doors for these beings, allowing them to attach to you and feed upon your energies. These images can be cleansed as well, but with a little different approach.

In the case of positive images, you feel positive emotions — if the image is allowing an entity to feed upon you, it needs to be cleansed. You can do this through a standard procedure, with a small difference to points 3 and 4. Instead of saying that you "feel good, relaxed, calm, secured," say and feel that you're neutral and calm, and that positive emotions are leaving. Say, "I'm no longer accepting these emotions; I'm no longer allowing access; I'm closed to these entities." The point is to change positive emotions into neutral emotions — not negative, but neutral. Your subconscious must know that you're closed for anything that might be attached to these specific core images.

After a few weeks of working with core images, you might notice a difference. Your approach to life might be more positive, and your psychic sensitivity might increase while your psychic abilities might begin to awaken, etc. But it doesn't matter why you want to work with the core images. You might want to increase your psychic abilities or get out of debt. In any case, the effort of your work is worth it.

About the Author

Wojciech "Nathaniel" Usarzewicz is a Reiki practitioner and psychic who lives and practices in Poland. He's written numerous books about psychic development, runes, the New Age, and Reiki. He used to research haunted places in Poland; today he teaches Reiki and psychic development.

He maintains the English-based website, *A State of Mind* (http://astateofmind.eu), where he publishes articles about psychic abilities and spiritual growth.

Nathan can be contacted via e-mail: nathan@astateofmind.eu

Bibliography

— Baginski, B., Sharamon, S., The Chakra Handbook. Lotus Press, 1998.
— Belanger, M., *The Psychic Energy Codex: A Manual For Developing Your Subtle Senses.* Weiser Books, 2007.
— Caudill, M., *Suddenly Psychic: A Skeptic's Journey.* Hampton Roads Pub Co, 2006.
— Greer, J.M., *The New Encyclopedia of the Occult.* Llewellyn Publications, 2003.
— Guiley, R.E., *The Encyclopedia of Ghosts and Spirits.* Facts On File, 2007.
— Nathaniel, *Psychic Development Simplified.* A State of Mind, 2011.
— Tabis, E.K., Zadlo, L., *Rozwijanie zdolnosci parapsychicznych*. Ravi, 1994.
— Tertre, du, N., *Psychic Intuition.* Self-publishing, 2010.
— Ward, T. Discover Your Psychic Powers. Arcturus Publishing, 2008.
— Zadlo, L., *Jak korzystac ze zdolnosci parapsychicznych*. Sadhana, 1997.

And check out other books by Nathaniel on Amazon
http://www.amazon.com/-/e/B005B63BDQ

Lightning Source UK Ltd.
Milton Keynes UK
UKHW02f1941230518
323110UK00035B/472/P